The future of social housing

Edited by Suzanne Fitzpatrick
and Mark Stephens

Acknowledgments

The editors are extremely grateful to all the
contributors for managing to produce their
chapters to an exceptionally tight timescale.
We would also like to thank Caroline Davey,
Deputy Director of Communications, Policy and
Campaigns at Shelter, for her excellent support
and advice throughout the process of putting
together this edited volume. Nicola Hawthorne,
of the Centre for Housing Policy, University
of York, provided invaluable assistance in
preparing the manuscript for submission to
Shelter, for which we are also very grateful.

Disclaimer

All views and any errors contained in the book
are the responsibility of the relevant authors.

Printed in the UK by CPI William Clowes,
Beccles NR34 7TL
Typeset by Image Creative Design

Published by Shelter
88 Old Street
London EC1V 9HU
0845 458 4590
www.shelter.org.uk

Registered charity in England and Wales (263710) and
in Scotland (SC002327).

RH 1893

Everyone should have a home
Shelter, the housing and
homelessness charity

Foreword

In 2007, the Government made a commitment to build three million additional new homes by 2020, and specifically to increase the number of social rented homes. This was welcome news, and something for which Shelter had long campaigned. After decades of under-investment in social housing – which has led to a severe backlog of unmet housing need – we see on a daily basis the impact that this chronic shortage of social rented homes has on our clients.

Importantly, this commitment was made in the context of an explicit recognition that the increase in social housing supply will have to go hand-in-hand with reform, to ensure best use is made of these homes. Indeed, Professor John Hills' 2007 review, *Ends and means: the future roles of social housing in England*[1], has prefigured a debate about the role and purpose of social housing, as well as the rights and responsibilities of its current and future tenants. This debate has ranged far and wide over the last 18 months, taking in everything from quality and choice to neighbourhoods and employment.

Throughout this debate – and in the run-up to the launch of a Housing Reform Green Paper in late 2008 – Shelter has been keen to ensure that arguments and discussions about social housing are grounded in a robust evidence base. A conversation with Suzanne Fitzpatrick back in December 2007 set the ball rolling on this project, and I am indebted to her and Mark Stephens for inviting a range of eminent academics, from across six universities, to contribute a chapter on their specialist areas to this volume. The expertise and independence of all of the contributing authors adds enormous weight to the book, and we thank them for giving their time to this project so freely.

Collectively, Shelter believes that these individual chapters make a powerful case for a renewed and reinvigorated social housing sector. The message that comes through loud and clear is this: social rented housing plays an invaluable role in tackling poverty and meeting housing need, and in order to provide housing fit for the twenty-first century we must build on the sector's many strengths as well as tackling its systemic weaknesses.

The evidence presented here demonstrates that the shortage of supply is a principal weakness of the existing social housing sector. The inadequacy of supply in meeting housing need has had a range of negative effects; most notably, the necessary rationing has meant that allocations have been

---

[1] Hills, J., 2007. *Ends and means: the future roles of social housing in England.* CASE Report 34, London: CASE and LSE. Available at: http://tinyurl.com/24ms5b

prioritised to those who are most vulnerable and in greatest housing need, leading in many areas to spatially concentrated disadvantage.

Clearly, the current economic downturn is having a damaging effect on output in the short term; in recent months an alarming number of housebuilders have laid off staff, mothballed projects, and revised output projections downwards. And as more households get into financial difficulties – whether through rising food and fuel bills, higher mortgage costs, or unemployment – it is likely that demand for social housing will rise even further. Despite these market difficulties, it is plain that we must build substantially more social housing. It must be the priority of both the public and private housing sectors, to ensure that the delivery of social rented housing is maximised in the coming years.

Beyond the need for *more* social housing, there is clearly work to be done to address the sector's weaknesses, while retaining its core strengths. A number of themes about the sector's strengths emerge from this volume: that social housing's 'safety net' role for homeless households provides a vital legal framework without parallel in other countries; that recent efforts to improve the quality of social housing are a welcome step in ensuring that it provides decent homes from which tenants have a secure base to improve their lives; and that security of tenure is a cornerstone of social housing's benefits for tenants. Indeed, there is a striking consensus among the contributors to this volume that security of tenure plays a fundamental role in social housing, and that dismantling it would be actively damaging to the life chances of tenants, including their ability to find and keep work. In light of ongoing discussions about social housing reform, this support for security of tenure from a range of academic experts comes at a vitally important time.

Equally, themes emerge about areas for reform; it is clear that more creative solutions need to be found to locate social housing within mixed communities, both for new developments and also for the existing stock. There is also a need for tailored and incentives-based approaches to tackling worklessness in social housing – including addressing the disincentives of in-work Housing Benefit – which will be more effective than a punitive or conditional approach.

At Shelter we welcome the debate on how best to reform the social housing sector for the twenty-first century, but this debate must be grounded in two key principles: the first priority must be to increase social housing supply; and, secondly, social housing currently has a series of key strengths which must be preserved. Ultimately, social rented housing is an enormous – and, in many respects, unique – asset to our housing system, and we must take the opportunity of the current debate and forthcoming Green Paper to shape social housing's future so that it continues to play this role for the many existing and future tenants who need it.

Adam Sampson
Shelter Chief Executive

Contents

Chapter 1

Housing: the saving grace in the British welfare state?

Jonathan Bradshaw, Yekaterina Chzhen and Mark Stephens

Background

In 1987, in Thatcherite days, Bradshaw and Holmes (1989) conducted a study of 67 couples with dependent children in Tyne and Wear living on Supplementary Benefit. The study was motivated by the anxiety of the Millfield Foundation, a local trust, about the effects on the unemployed of living long-term on social assistance. At the time, unemployment in Tyne and Wear was 16 per cent – nearly double the national average. The study was a very intensive investigation involving repeated interviews, an inventory of household possessions, and the completion by all members of the family of diaries relating to time, activities and travel. Its main conclusion was that the rates of Supplementary Benefit were grossly too low (and were just about to be cut further on the introduction of Income Support in 1988).

> 'The picture that emerges from this detailed study of family lives is one of constant restriction in almost every aspect of people's activities… The lives of these families, and perhaps most seriously the lives of the children in them, are marked by the unrelieved struggle to manage, with dreary diets and drab clothing. They suffer what amounts to cultural imprisonment in their home…' (Bradshaw and Holmes 1989, p.138.)

However, there was one element in their lives that provided some mitigation – housing.

> 'One of the major determinants of the level of living of families is the standard of their housing. The majority of the families in our sample lived in modern council housing: they were not overcrowded, none lacked basic amenities, all had gardens and few defects were reported. The housing was mainly satisfactory, and the families were generally satisfied with their housing, though relatively high proportions complained of draughts and poor insulation. There was also considerable dissatisfaction with heating… They emphasise the importance of housing policies providing good standard low rent housing in alleviating the experience of poverty.' (Ibid, p.133.)

Fast-forward 20 years to something completely different – a comparative study of child wellbeing in the European Union (Bradshaw et al 2007). The study made an assessment of child wellbeing on eight dimensions: material situation, health, education, subjective wellbeing, risk and safety, personal and family relationships, citizenship, and housing and the environment. In Figure 1, below, it can be seen that the UK came towards the bottom of the overall league table, just above Latvia, Estonia and Lithuania, but below countries such as Portugal, Hungary, and the Czech and Slovak Republics. For a rich country, the UK did pretty badly across almost all of the domains. But one domain it did not do badly on was housing and neighbourhood, and within housing and neighbourhood it did comparatively very well on housing.

Figure 1: Child wellbeing in the EU

	Average rank	Health	Subjective wellbeing	Children's relationships	Material situation	Risk and safety	Education	Civic and political participation	Housing
Cyprus	4.6	5			1	2		1	14
Netherlands	4.9	2	1	5	10	5	6		5
Sweden	5.9	1	6	16	2	3	2	14	4
Denmark	6.4	3	9	10	6	15	3		1
Spain	8.7	13	3	9	8	1	15	4	1
Finland	9.8	7	12	17	3	7	4	18	10
Germany	9.9	10	7	12	12	12	9	10	7
Belgium	10.4	20	15	6	18	16	1	5	2
Slovenia	10.7	15	8	4	4	13		15	13
Ireland	12.1	18	5	8	19	20	7		8
Italy	12.3	16	11	2	15	6	19	11	18
Luxembourg	12.4	11	20	10	5	9	20		3
Greece	12.5	25	4	11	17	8	18	2	17
Austria	12.6	21	2	18	7	19	17		6
Portugal	12.9	9	16	3	13	17	18	7	20
France	13.0	14	13	14	11	10	14		15
Poland	13.0	6	19	13	23	11	5	6	21
Hungary	13.0	22	10	7	14	14	12	3	22
Malta	13.5	24	17	1	24	4			11
Czech Republic	14.1	4	14	22	9	21	10	17	16
Slovak Republic	16.6	17	22		25	13	11	9	19
United Kingdom	17.0	23	18	23	20	22	13	8	9
Latvia	17.6	19	21	18	16	23	8	12	24
Estonia	19.9	12	23	21	21	24		15	23
Lithuania	20.0	8	24	20	22	25		16	25

Note: 1 = best

Source: Bradshaw et al (2007).

These two findings, from different studies and separated by 20 years, led us to ask the question: does good quality housing represent a hidden asset (for poor people) in the UK? In the standard comparisons of poverty rates, the UK does badly – for example, it comes seventeenth in the official league table of EU27 child poverty rates in 2005 (European Commission 2008, Figure 1a). In the comparative literature on welfare state regimes we do not do well (http://tinyurl.com/6qb249). But housing is absent from the most influential academic work on welfare regimes (Esping-Andersen 1990), and even in housing studies literature its importance is often played down and it is characterised as the 'wobbly pillar of the welfare state' (Torgersen 1987).

A key part of this housing and poverty 'story' in the UK, and the focus of this book, is the social rented sector. Although social housing now accommodates only 17 per cent of the population, it contains 39 per cent of the UK's households that live in poverty (defined as having incomes less than 60 per cent of the median after housing costs) and 44 per cent of poor children in the UK in 2005/06 (Department for Work and Pensions (DWP) 2007). The child poverty rate is much higher in social housing than in other tenures – 60 per cent, compared with 17 per cent for owners with a mortgage and 49 per cent in private rented housing. But do those poor families have the saving grace of good quality housing? Is that saving grace a characteristic of the British welfare state – something perhaps we should be proud about and concerned to protect?

This chapter seeks to answer this question by reviewing the evidence on housing conditions in the UK, compared to other European countries, with a particular focus on poorer groups and those living in the social rented sector.

There aren't very many, or particularly good, sources of comparative data on housing.[1] The main source in this chapter is the one we used for the housing domain in the child wellbeing index – the *European Quality of Life Survey* (Euroqual, 2003).[2] In the following sections we compare countries' housing quality using three broad domains:

- space standards (the detailed criteria are rooms per person, and perceived shortage of space)

- standards of repair (the detailed criteria are rot in windows/doors/floors, and damp and leaks) and

- perceived safety in the local area.

We are able to analyse variation in these categories, within and between countries, according to:

- income quintile

- tenure, and

- household type.

Income quintile is based on grouped net household income data. We have used households' equivalent income in euros, following the modified Organisation for Economic Co-operation and Development (OECD) scale, in order to take account of household size and economies of scale. Quintile 1 is the poorest and 5 is the richest in the analysis below. With regards to tenure, our key focus is the social rented sector, but the analysis also provides results for homeowners, private tenants, and those who live

---

[1] The last wave of the European Community Household Panel was in 2001 and had rather limited housing data (though what there is in the 1998 panel is presented by Stephens and Lynch (2005)). We did not have access to the first wave of the new *EU Survey of Income and Living Conditions* (2004).

[2] This is a general purpose survey, run every four years by the European Foundation for the Improvement of Working and Living Conditions in Dublin. It is a questionnaire-based household survey based on representative samples of the population in each of 25 countries in the EU, as well as in Romania, Bulgaria and Turkey. The survey we used was for 2003, the most recent one was not yet available (2007).

rent-free or in other unusual arrangements. The household types considered include 'childless non-pensioner households' (no children under 16, no adults above 60), 'families with children' (children under 16 present), and 'pensioner households' (no children under 16, adults above 60 present). We have restricted analysis to the EU15 – the countries that were members of the EU before May 2004.

Space standards

Rooms per person

Figure 2, below, compares the average rooms per person. It shows that the UK comes second only to Belgium on this element of housing quality.

Figure 2: Average rooms per person in EU15 (2003)

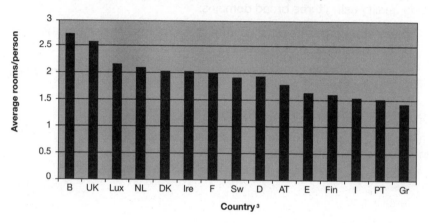

In Figure 3, opposite, we find that the UK comes top of the league table for households in the bottom quintile and, while in most countries average rooms per person diminishes with each income quintile, in the UK there is a U-shaped relationship with income – average rooms per person is highest at the bottom and top of the distribution.

---

[3] AT = Austria, B = Belgium, D = Germany, DK = Denmark, E = Spain, F = France, Fin = Finland, Gr = Greece, Ire = Ireland, I = Italy, Lux = Luxembourg, NL = Netherlands, PT = Portugal, Sw = Sweden, UK = United Kingdom.

Figure 3: Average rooms per person across income quintiles in EU15 (2003)

	Income quintile					
	1	2	3	4	5	Average
Belgium	2.5	2.6	2.9	2.4	3.2	2.7
UK	**2.8**	**2.5**	**2.3**	**2.7**	**2.9**	**2.6**
Netherlands	1.7	2.2	2.1	2.4	2.4	2.2
Denmark	1.9	2.0	1.9	2.0	2.2	2.0
Luxembourg	1.6	1.9	2.2	2.1	2.8	2.1
Ireland	2.0	2.0	2.0	2.1	2.4	2.1
Germany	1.9	1.8	1.8	1.9	2.2	1.9
France	1.6	1.9	2.2	2.1	2.3	2.0
Sweden	1.7	1.8	2.0	2.0	2.1	1.9
Austria	1.6	1.9	1.7	1.8	2.1	1.8
Spain	1.8	1.6	1.6	1.5	2.1	1.7
Finland	1.5	1.7	1.4	1.6	1.8	1.6
Portugal	1.6	1.5	1.5	1.7	1.5	1.6
Italy	1.1	1.5	1.7	1.6	1.9	1.5
Greece	1.4	1.3	1.3	1.3	1.6	1.4

In Figure 4, below, there are no significant differences in average rooms per person across types of housing tenure in the UK. However, tenants in the social rented sector have the highest space standards on this measure, after Luxembourg.

Figure 4: Average rooms per person across tenure types in EU15 (2003)[4]

	Tenure type				
	Own	Rent privately	Social rent	Rent-free/other	Average
Belgium	2.8	2.6	2.3	2.7	2.7
UK	**2.6**	**2.4**	**2.6**	**2.8**	**2.6**
Luxembourg	2.2	1.9	2.8	2.4	2.1
Netherlands	2.0	2.2	2.2	1.5	2.1
Ireland	2.2	1.5	1.7	2.0	2.0
Denmark	2.2	1.8	1.7	2.0	2.0
France	2.2	1.9	1.6	1.7	2.0
Germany	2.2	1.7	1.6	1.9	1.9
Sweden	2.1	1.7	1.7	2.0	1.9
Austria	1.9	1.7	1.5	2.0	1.8
Spain	1.7	1.5	1.6	1.9	1.6
Finland	1.7	1.4	1.4	1.8	1.6
Italy	1.6	1.5	1.3	1.5	1.5
Portugal	1.6	1.4	1.4	1.5	1.5
Greece	1.5	1.3	1.2	1.4	1.4

[4] Country proportions in the 'Average' column may differ from the corresponding figures in Figure 3 because of the missing values of the income variable.

There were significant differences in average rooms per person across household types in all countries. Comparing the room standards between countries, one of the reasons for the high UK room standard is the position of pensioner households who have the third highest number of rooms per person and the childless, non-pensioner households who have the second highest (see Figure 5, below). The UK does not do so well for families with children but still comes equal fifth with Ireland, Germany and Sweden.

Figure 5: Average rooms per person across household types in EU15 (2003)

	Household type			
	No children under 16, no adults above 60	Children under 16 present[5]	No children under 16, adults above 60 present	Average
Belgium	2.9	1.6	3.5	2.7
UK	**2.5**	**1.2**	**2.8**	**2.6**
Luxembourg	2.4	1.3	2.9	2.2
Netherlands	2.3	1.3	2.6	2.1
Ireland	2.2	1.2	2.7	2.0
Denmark	2.1	1.3	2.5	2.0
France	2.0	1.1	2.6	2.0
Germany	2.0	1.2	2.2	1.9
Sweden	1.9	1.2	2.6	1.9
Austria	1.9	1.1	2.2	1.8
Spain	1.7	1.0	2.0	1.6
Finland	1.7	1.1	1.9	1.6
Italy	1.6	0.9	1.9	1.5
Portugal	1.6	0.9	1.9	1.5
Greece	1.6	0.9	1.6	1.4

Perceived shortage of space

The second indicator of housing quality is the proportion of households who report shortage of space – it is a more subjective indicator of overcrowding. On this indicator the UK does not do so well, coming twelfth in Figure 6, opposite.

---

[5] According to the *European Quality of Life Survey* (EQLS) *Fieldwork Technical Report* (August 2003), the percentage of children under 16 was too low in the UK, and this data problem had not been resolved by EQLS technicians (p.37). Therefore, any analysis by household type with respect to the UK has to be interpreted with caution.

Figure 6: Percentage of households that report shortage of space in EU15 (2003)

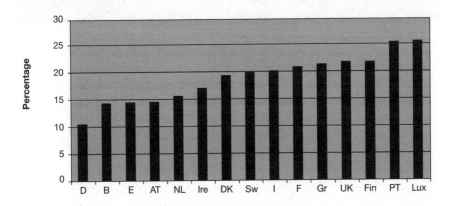

However, in Figure 7, below, the UK comes much further up the league table for the lowest quintile group (third), and the differences in the percentage reporting shortage of space do not vary significantly for the UK while they do, falling with income quintile, in many of the other countries.

Figure 7: Percentage of households that report shortage of space across income quintiles in EU15 (2003)

	Income quintile					
	1	2	3	4	5	Average
Germany	10.3	18.1	9.4	5.7	8.6	10.6
Belgium	24.3	16.1	11.8	16.5	14.4	16.6
Spain	17.4	14.7	14.8	13.9	11.2	14.3
Austria	24.5	13.9	16.2	14.9	7.6	15.4
Netherlands	25.5	21.1	10.1	11.6	9.9	15.8
Ireland	24.4	36.3	16.5	11.0	4.6	19.0
Denmark	22.2	19.4	23.2	17.1	18.3	20.1
Sweden	30.3	22.4	17.6	14.6	16.1	20.1
Italy	39.8	20.2	19.8	20.9	9.8	22.2
France	23.6	20.5	25.8	20.1	18.1	21.7
Greece	21.8	34.4	20.5	23.2	21.1	23.7
UK	**18.3**	**25.5**	**25.6**	**16.1**	**25.2**	**22.0**
Finland	24.3	19.0	27.2	23.3	21.8	23.0
Portugal	37.6	30.9	28.7	24.1	12.0	26.2
Luxembourg	36.1	34.3	31.1	31.9	28.9	32.3

Similarly, perceived shortage of space does not vary across tenure groups in the UK, (see Figure 8, overleaf) unlike in many other countries, as it comes sixth from top of the league table for social housing.

Figure 8: Percentage of households that report shortage of space across tenure types in EU15 (2003)

	Tenure type				
	Own	Rent privately	Social rent	Rent-free/other	Average
Germany	3.2	15.3	18.6	19.2	10.6
Belgium	8.9	33.8	28.9	5.2	14.4
Spain	12.4	20.5	16.7	22.5	14.3
Austria	7.0	24.0	22.3	18.0	14.5
Netherlands	11.3	16.9	20.2	17.5	15.6
Ireland	11.0	21.0	46.9	24.1	16.9
Denmark	14.3	28.5	29.3	20.4	19.4
Sweden	15.1	27.4	25.4	21.4	19.6
Italy	17.2	33.6	17.3	31.6	20.1
France	10.5	30.9	29.8	28.9	20.8
Greece	18.5	26.9	28.6	29.0	21.3
UK	**21.9**	**21.1**	**21.8**	**18.2**	**21.7**
Finland	20.0	31.5	20.5	15.0	21.7
Portugal	17.2	41.5	35.4	23.6	25.2
Luxembourg	24.0	34.0	22.2	16.0	25.3

The reason for the relatively poor overall UK ranking on shortage of space seems to be mainly down to the circumstances of families with children who come bottom of the league (see Figure 9, below).

Figure 9: Percentage of households that report shortage of space across household types in EU15 (2003)

	Household type			
	No children under 16, no adults above 60	Children under 16 present	No children under 16, adults above 60 present	Average
Germany	12.3	21.5	3.1	10.5
Belgium	15.4	20.4	7.6	14.4
Spain	13.5	26.4	6.2	14.4
Austria	15.3	23.8	6.6	14.6
Netherlands	16.2	22.1	6.8	15.6
Ireland	17.0	22.9	10.0	17.1
Denmark	21.0	29.7	8.5	19.3
Sweden	23.4	31.6	4.8	19.8
Italy	22.0	31.7	11.0	20.1
France	24.4	31.7	6.2	20.8
Greece	21.6	26.8	17.4	21.3
UK	**24.5**	**54.2**	**12.2**	**21.6**
Finland	19.2	41.0	9.8	21.8
Portugal	20.9	34.4	20.4	25.3
Luxembourg	26.3	30.9	17.5	25.5

State of repair

Rot in windows, doors and floors

This is one of two indicators we have on state of repair. Overall, in Figure 10, below, the UK comes seventh in the percentage of households reporting rot in windows, doors and floors.

Figure 10: Percentage of households that report rot in windows, doors, floors in EU15 (2003)

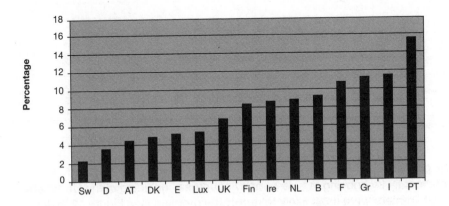

Perhaps not surprisingly, rot is more prevalent in the lowest income quintile (see Figure 11, overleaf) in most countries, but the UK does slightly better than average with the bottom quintile coming seventh.

Figure 11: Percentage of households that report rot in windows, doors, floors across income quintiles in EU15 (2003)

| | Income quintile | | | | | |
	1	2	3	4	5	Average
Sweden	4.6	2.8	1.6	1.8	1.6	2.4
Germany	4.7	5.0	5.7	1.3	2.3	3.8
Austria	8.0	5.9	2.8	6.0	1.4	4.9
Denmark	3.5	8.8	5.2	3.2	3.8	4.9
Spain	13.6	9.3	0.8	1.4	3.5	5.7
Luxembourg	6.2	9.6	2.7	4.2	1.3	4.7
UK	**12.0**	**6.6**	**6.3**	**2.8**	**3.3**	**6.3**
Finland	11.1	7.3	7.7	10.6	5.8	8.5
Ireland	18.6	15.5	11.1	8.8	2.3	11.4
Netherlands	13.8	7.8	8.1	9.0	5.3	8.8
Belgium	17.1	12.8	10.4	9.0	4.8	10.8
France	13.0	10.8	9.9	8.5	6.1	9.7
Greece	25.5	20.9	9.4	8.8	4.1	13.1
Italy	16.5	18.0	11.2	10.2	4.0	12.1
Portugal	26.2	22.3	22.1	15.4	6.0	18.0

The probability of reporting rot in windows, doors or floors varied significantly by housing tenure in many countries, including in the UK where private renters were most likely to report the problem (see Figure 12, below). In comparative terms, the UK's performance is average in its social rented tenure, coming eighth in the league table overall.

Figure 12: Percentage of households that report rot in windows, doors, floors across tenure types in EU15 (2003)

| | Tenure type | | | | |
	Own	Rent privately	Social rent	Rent-free/other	Average
Sweden	1.5	3.8	2.3	3.8	2.2
Germany	1.1	6.3	5.2	0	3.6
Austria	3.1	4.2	6.2	9.8	4.5
Denmark	3.7	8.1	6.6	7.4	5.0
Spain	3.3	11.2	12.0	15.0	5.3
Luxembourg	4.2	9.9	0	13.8	5.5
UK	**3.9**	**15.7**	**8.8**	**13.6**	**6.9**
Finland	7.2	18.6	4.2	15.8	8.5
Ireland	5.7	8.9	27.4	14.3	8.9
Netherlands	8.0	21.7	8.7	2.5	8.8
Belgium	4.3	20.1	25.6	15.5	9.3
France	5.0	13.6	20.2	15.8	10.7
Greece	12.4	6.7	42.9	21.9	11.3
Italy	6.2	28.0	32.1	26.3	11.5
Portugal	8.4	27.8	26.8	19.1	15.6

There was no significant association between the likelihood of reporting rot in windows, doors or floors and household type in the UK. Only in Germany, Netherlands and Belgium, where families with children were most likely to report rot, and in Greece and Portugal, where pensioner households were most likely to report the problem, was a significant association with household type observed.

Figure 13: Percentage of households that report rot in windows, doors, floors across household types in EU15 (2003)

	Household type			
	No children under 16, no adults above 60	Children under 16 present	No children under 16, adults above 60 present	Average
Sweden	2.9	3.0	1.0	2.3
Germany	3.5	7.2	2.3	3.7
Austria	4.8	3.6	5.0	4.6
Denmark	5.0	7.1	3.2	4.9
Spain	4.5	6.6	5.1	5.3
Luxembourg	7.1	4.0	5.4	5.5
UK	7.5	8.3	5.1	6.8
Finland	9.6	8.5	6.7	8.5
Ireland	7.3	9.0	10.8	8.7
Netherlands	8.0	13.1	5.6	8.8
Belgium	11.1	11.3	5.0	9.3
France	11.4	12.6	8.3	10.8
Greece	6.6	13.0	15.5	11.3
Italy	9.7	13.5	12.1	11.6
Portugal	11.4	13.8	21.5	15.6

Damp and leaks

The second variable for housing conditions is damp and leaks. In Figure 14, below, the UK comes fourth from best when looking at this variable.

Figure 14: Percentage of households that report damp/leaks in EU15 (2003)

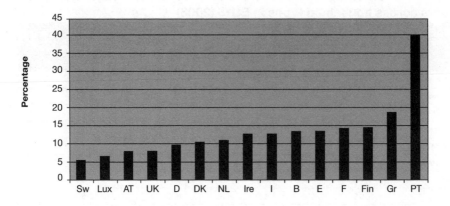

The probability of reporting damp/leaks varied significantly with income in the UK and a number of other countries (see Figure 15, below), with households from lower income quintiles more likely to report the problem. The UK comes seventh with respect to the bottom quintile.

Figure 15: Percentage of households that report damp/leaks across income quintiles in EU15 (2003)

	Income quintile					
	1	2	3	4	5	Average
Sweden	4.6	8.3	5.9	3.5	5.2	5.5
Luxembourg	12.3	16.4	2.7	7.1	3.9	8.4
Austria	14.6	8.6	4.2	5.9	5.5	7.8
UK	**14.8**	**10.2**	**7.0**	**4.9**	**5.7**	**8.6**
Germany	12.1	14.9	10.1	5.7	6.9	10.0
Denmark	10.5	13.5	9.8	7.6	10.0	10.3
Netherlands	13.0	13.9	13.1	12.9	7.9	12.2
Ireland	25.6	27.2	15.4	12.2	3.4	17.0
Italy	27.6	18.8	10.3	7.8	1.6	13.3
Belgium	20.0	19.2	16.7	14.3	10.3	16.0
Spain	22.7	10.1	9.0	14.0	13.3	13.9
France	24.5	14.7	15.3	10.4	8.1	14.7
Finland	19.3	11.0	15.6	13.4	13.8	14.5
Greece	29.1	29.3	22.0	13.4	16.5	21.7
Portugal	52.0	51.8	50.0	38.3	23.8	42.6

The probability of reporting damp/leaks varied significantly by housing tenure in the UK (see Figure 16, below), with those living rent-free and private renters most likely to report the problem. The pattern across European countries was mixed. Social renters were more likely to report the problem in some countries (eg Ireland), while private renters were in others (eg Portugal). But social renters in the UK came second to top of the league table.

Figure 16: Percentage of households that report damp/leaks across tenure types in EU15 (2003)

	Tenure type				
	Own	Rent privately	Social rent	Rent-free/other	Average
Sweden	5.4	6.6	3.0	8.0	5.4
Luxembourg	6.1	9.0	10.0	6.9	6.7
Austria	6.8	10.2	9.0	6.6	7.9
UK	**5.7**	**16.5**	**8.1**	**18.2**	**8.0**
Germany	5.1	13.1	15.5	0	9.6
Denmark	4.5	18.5	20.2	25.9	10.5
Netherlands	6.3	20.0	15.6	5.3	11.0
Ireland	8.1	18.7	36.3	13.8	12.9
Italy	9.7	21.4	20.8	26.3	12.6
Belgium	8.1	27.9	28.9	15.5	13.5
Spain	10.2	25.3	12.5	25.0	13.4
France	7.6	21.1	19.6	23.1	14.4
Finland	14.7	17.0	8.4	40.0	14.5
Greece	17.0	20.6	71.4	22.6	18.6
Portugal	28.2	61.4	50.0	50.0	40.0

The probability of reporting damp/leaks varied significantly by household type in the UK, with childless, non-pensioner households most likely to report the problem. For families with children the UK came top of the league table in Figure 17, overleaf.

Figure 17: Percentage of households that report damp/leaks across household types in EU15 (2003)

	Household type			
	No children under 16, no adults above 60	Children under 16 present	No children under 16, adults above 60 present	Average
Sweden	6.2	6.0	3.9	5.4
Luxembourg	5.6	7.6	6.6	6.6
Austria	7.6	7.7	8.3	7.8
UK	**9.7**	**4.2**	**4.4**	**8.0**
Germany	9.4	14.3	8.2	9.8
Denmark	13.8	11.4	3.6	10.4
Netherlands	12.4	15.0	3.6	11.0
Ireland	10.7	14.0	14.4	12.6
Italy	11.3	14.2	13.1	12.7
Belgium	14.3	16.3	9.2	13.3
Spain	13.0	15.1	13.0	13.5
France	14.8	18.1	10.7	14.4
Finland	14.4	18.0	12.0	14.6
Greece	16.2	22.6	19.1	18.7
Portugal	31.1	41.3	46.8	39.8

Safety in the local area

The quality of neighbourhood indicator we have is feelings about safety in the local area. Figure 18, below, shows that the UK does not generally perform well on this indicator, coming second from bottom overall.

Figure 18: Percentage of households that think that it is unsafe or very unsafe to walk around in their area at night in EU15 (2003)

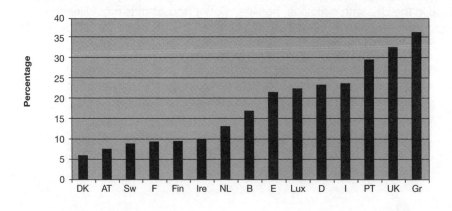

There is a highly significant variation by quintile group in the UK, and feelings of safety are comparatively much worse among lower quintile groups in Figure 19, opposite.

Figure 19: Percentage of households that think that it is unsafe or very unsafe to walk around in their area at night across income quintiles in EU15 (2003)

	Income quintile					
	1	2	3	4	5	Average
Denmark	11.1	8.8	4.6	3.8	1.4	5.8
Austria	11.9	7.5	7.8	4.8	7.0	7.8
Sweden	10.8	13.2	10.2	5.8	3.1	8.6
France	15.0	12.7	10.5	9.7	4.0	10.5
Finland	12.7	10.6	8.8	8.9	5.3	9.2
Ireland	23.5	18.0	6.7	5.6	3.5	11.6
Netherlands	18.4	15.8	13.8	12.8	7.9	13.8
Belgium	26.3	23.0	15.2	18.0	11.0	18.4
Spain	28.7	25.0	21.5	22.7	16.8	22.8
Luxembourg	32.3	24.3	20.5	10.3	17.6	20.8
Germany	34.1	28.5	26.3	17.1	15.6	24.4
Italy	32.5	31.0	28.8	13.4	15.7	24.2
Portugal	31.9	43.8	20.5	28.4	27.8	30.2
UK	50.7	41.4	35.0	17.7	18.7	32.9
Greece	30.0	45.1	37.6	37.8	36.4	37.1

The European data suggests that there is no significant association between the probability of reporting lack of safety in their area at night and housing tenure in the UK (see Figure 20, below).

Figure 20: Percentage of households that think that it is unsafe or very unsafe to walk around in their area at night across tenure types in EU15 (2003)

	Tenure type				
	Own	Rent privately	Social rent	Rent-free/other	Average
Denmark	4.3	9.8	10.6	1.9	6.1
Austria	5.3	6.0	13.2	6.7	7.6
Sweden	4.4	15.7	16.4	10.7	8.9
France	4.2	12.3	19.5	7.7	9.4
Finland	8.2	9.4	14.8	15.0	9.6
Ireland	7.0	11.5	23.9	14.3	9.7
Netherlands	7.3	28.3	18.3	7.7	13.1
Belgium	14.3	22.1	34.1	10.7	17.1
Spain	21.3	23.2	12.5	20.5	21.4
Luxembourg	23.6	19.6	10.0	17.9	22.4
Germany	16.7	25.4	37.2	15.4	23.4
Italy	21.1	28.7	48.1	24.3	23.7
Portugal	25.8	38.1	37.0	23.3	29.5
UK	30.6	41.6	33.1	27.3	32.6
Greece	35.6	38.5	14.3	31.3	36.1

However, more reliable English data suggests that there is a very strong association between perceptions of safety and tenure, with social tenants the most fearful (see Figure 21, below).

Figure 21: Percentage of households not feeling safe alone by tenure (2004) (England)

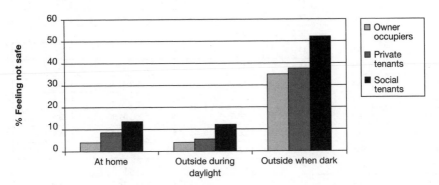

Source: English House Condition Survey 2004.

The European data does suggest a significant association between the probability of reporting lack of safety and household type in the UK, with families with children, followed by pensioner households, most likely to report lack of safety in their local area at night (see Figure 22, opposite).

Figure 22: Percentage of households that think that it is unsafe or very unsafe to walk around in their area at night across household types in EU15 (2003)

	Household type			
	No children under 16, no adults above 60	Children under 16 present	No children under 16, adults above 60 present	Average
Denmark	3.0	4.3	12.5	5.9
Austria	7.5	3.6	10.5	7.6
Sweden	7.2	5.6	14.1	8.9
France	7.9	10.0	11.7	9.4
Finland	7.7	6.3	15.4	9.6
Ireland	7.6	13.7	9.3	9.9
Netherlands	11.0	10.7	20.5	13.1
Belgium	14.7	11.7	24.8	16.9
Spain	17.9	23.2	24.1	21.5
Luxembourg	16.7	17.4	36.5	22.3
Germany	18.9	16.1	32.3	23.3
Italy	16.5	23.4	30.5	23.6
Portugal	28.6	28.3	31.8	29.6
UK	**27.6**	**50.0**	**43.4**	**32.6**
Greece	31.5	30.9	44.8	36.2

Conclusion

The conclusion from this analysis is that the hypothesis that the UK has a saving grace in the quality of its housing can only be upheld with some reservations. Certainly the UK does comparatively very well on rooms per person. However, it does less well on perceived shortage of space and on rot, damp and leaks, and it does not do at all well on feelings of safety in the local area.

However, in some of these indicators where it does not do particularly well there is less variation by income quintile in the UK than elsewhere – the lowest quintile is not much more worse-off. Also, social housing is often similar to, or even better than, other tenures, especially the private rented sector. There is a mixed picture by family type, though families with children tend to do worse on most indicators.

The UK certainly does better on these housing indicators than it did on most poverty league tables in 2003. So housing is a comparative asset.

The explanation for these relatively good housing outcomes for poorer households in the UK are explored in Part 2 of the book in which the contribution of key housing policy instruments – social rented housing (Chapter 2), the statutory homelessness safety net (Chapter 3) and Housing Benefit (Chapter 4) – are examined.

Part 3 moves on to address the key problems associated with social housing that need to be acknowledged and addressed. These include social housing's contribution to the spatial segregation of poorer people (Chapter 5), concerns about the lack of choice in the social rented sector (Chapter 6), the high levels of worklessness among working-age social tenants (Chapter 7), the supply and quality of social rented housing (Chapter 8), and the nature of future demand for social housing (Chapter 9). Chapter 10 draws the various threads of argument underlying the book together and, in particular, identifies what the evidence reviewed suggests should be retained and changed about the social housing sector in this country. Several of the chapters address the question of security of tenure that has received much attention recently, but which has been regarded as an essential feature of social housing since its introduction in 1980 as one of the recommendations of the 1977 review of housing policy that enjoyed bi-partisan support.

The book was prompted in part by John Hills' seminal review of social housing in England (Hills 2007), but is not intended as a direct 'response' to Hills. Rather, it was conceived of as an opportunity for a wide range of academics from across a number of universities to contribute to the ongoing debate on the future of social housing. While the main focus of this book, as with the Hills' review, is England, of necessity much of the data and research considered is Britain- or UK-wide.

Jonathan Bradshaw is Professor of Social Policy and Associate Director of the Social Policy Research Unit, University of York.

Yekaterina Chzhen is a PhD student at the Department of Social Policy and Social Work, University of York.

Mark Stephens is Professor of European Housing and Assistant Director of the Centre for Housing Policy, University of York.

References

Bradshaw, J.R. and Holmes, H., 1989. *Living on the edge: a study of the living standards of families on benefit in Tyne and Wear.* Tyneside Child Poverty Action Group: London.

Bradshaw, J., Hoelscher, P. and Richardson, D., 2007. An index of child well-being in the European Union. *Journal of Social Indicators Research,* 80, p.133–177. Available at: http://tinyurl.com/6cesux

DWP, 2007. *Households below average incomes 1994/5–2005/6.* London: DWP. Available at: http://tinyurl.com/5o67lr

Esping-Andersen, G., 1990. *The three worlds of welfare capitalism.* Cambridge: Polity Press.

European Commission, 2008. *Child poverty and well-being in the EU: current status and the way forward.* Brussels: Directorate-General for Employment, Social Affairs and Equal Opportunities.

Hills, J., 2007. *Ends and means: the future roles of social housing in England.* CASE Report 34. London: CASE and LSE. Available at: http://tinyurl.com/24ms5b

Stephens, M. and Lynch, E., 2005. *The cost, quantity and quality of housing consumption in the UK: comparisons with other European Union countries.* York: Centre for Housing Policy.

Torgersen, U., 1987. Housing: the wobbly pillar under the welfare state. In Turner, B., Kemeny, J. and Lundqvist, L. eds. *Between state and market: housing in the post-industrial era.* Stockholm: Almqvist and Wicksell International, p.116-126.

Chapter 2

The role of the social rented sector

Mark Stephens

'I do think we need this national debate about the role of social housing in the 21st century.' Caroline Flint, Housing Minister, 2008

Introduction

The tone of today's debate about the future of the social rented sector was set in the early years of the current Government, and is propelled by evidence that tenure aspirations lie in home ownership, 'up to 90% of people say that home ownership is their preferred choice' (Department of the Environment, Transport and the Regions (DETR) and Department for Social Security (DSS) 2000, p.30). These aspirations underpin the Government's commitment to increase the proportion of households who are homeowners (or at least own a share in their home). This has been the most consistent part of government policy, with the commitment to extend home ownership being repeated in government policy papers (notably Office of the Deputy Prime Minister (ODPM) 2005) and a series of equity share schemes being devised to enable 'at least 80,000 households into home ownership by 2010, as well as providing up to 300,000 social housing tenants with an opportunity to buy a stake in their own home' (ODPM 2005, p.37).

In its early years, the Government also made it clear that it wished the private rented sector 'to grow and prosper', noting that the proportion of households living in the British sector were 'exceptionally low by comparison with most other developed countries' (DETR and DSS 2000, p.44). The Government's approach towards the private rented sector, following a largely unforeseen influx of investment through buy-to-let mortgages, has shifted towards directing its growth. But one thing is clear (if never actually stated): if the proportion of households who are either homeowners or who are private tenants are to grow, then the proportion of households who rent their properties from social landlords must fall. Yet, the 2007 Housing Green Paper appeared to mark a change in tenure priorities, with the aim to increase social housing production to 45,000 units per year by 2010/11 and 50,000 per year thereafter (Communities and Local Government (CLG) 2007).

The Government has been reluctant to state explicitly what it sees the future role of the sector as being. On the one hand, the Government 'do not believe that social housing should only be allocated to the poorest and most vulnerable members of the community' (DETR and DSS 2000, p.80). On the other hand, 'if social housing was available to anyone who wanted it, there is a risk that it could be denied to those who had no other choice' (ibid). Consequently, 'we believe that priority for social housing should generally continue to be given to people in greatest housing need... [but] there may be occasions when it is necessary and desirable, for some wider community benefit, to allow exceptions' (ibid).

This chapter seeks to identify the role of the English (and the wider UK) social rented sector by drawing on evidence from other advanced economies.[1] The bulk of the chapter places social rented housing in advanced economies in their wider social and economic context. Evidence on eligibility, allocations and the profiles of the tenants who live in the sector are used to identify its role in different countries. Such an approach helps us to better understand not only its role but the reasons behind the role that the sector plays in England. A discussion of the policy implications of the analysis is presented and followed by conclusions.

The roles of social rented housing

Social rented housing takes many organisational forms across the advanced economies. These range from direct ownership by local government in England (council housing); through arms-length public bodies, such as municipal housing companies (in Sweden and Germany); to housing associations (in Denmark, the Netherlands and England); and private landlords (in Germany and the United States). Different organisational forms co-exist in many countries (for example, housing associations and local authorities in England, or municipal housing companies, private landlords and housing associations in Germany), though in others one type of provider holds a near monopoly over social provision (such as housing associations in the Netherlands and Denmark, or municipal housing companies in Sweden). Social landlords are not all non-profit-making organisations; nor are they always in receipt of subsidies (especially where sectors are 'mature' and have low debts).

Although the sector is diverse, it is possible to identify two essential characteristics:

- rents are set by non-market criteria, which normally results in below market levels, and

- allocations are made by administrative criteria.

---

[1] The evidence is largely drawn from Stephens et al (2002) and Fitzpatrick and Stephens (2007).

A review of social rented housing in advanced economies suggests that it plays four essential roles. One of these functions – the supply function – lies in the sphere of production; the others lie in the sphere of its consumption.

The supply function

Historically, social rented housing performed a supply function, mostly in European countries (both capitalist and socialist) that emerged from the Second World War with extensive housing shortages, often caused by war damage, even where this was minimal by urbanisation and other demographic pressures. These mass social housebuilding programmes began and finished at different times in the post-war period.

As in England, these programmes tended to be scaled back once 'crude' shortages had been met. The downward pressure on new building was reinforced by budgetary pressures, spanning from the oil crisis of the 1970s to the entry conditions of the European monetary union in the 1990s and beyond.

However, it is notable that many countries sustain social housebuilding programmes that are absolutely and proportionately much larger than those found in England or other parts of the UK. For example, in 2005, only 17,200 social housing completions took place in England (Whitehead 2007), compared to almost 43,000 in France (Levy-Vroelant and Tutin 2007), and 67,000 in the Netherlands (Elsinga and Wassenberg 2007). When one takes into account the size of the populations, the differences become stark. Despite England's population being three times greater than the Netherlands', Dutch social housing production outstrips England's by a ratio of 3.9 to 1.

Figure 1: Changes in the size of the social rented sector

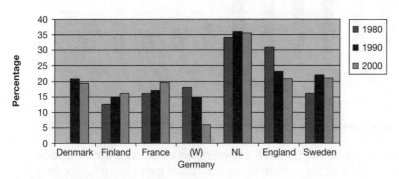

Source: Stephens et al (2002), Table 1.

Figure 1, above, shows changes in the size of social rented sectors in selected Western European countries between 1980 and 2000. The proportion of households living in social rented housing has shrunk enough to suggest a significant absolute decline in the sector in only two countries – England and Germany. These reductions have occurred as a matter of policy – for example, in England through the Right to Buy scheme and severe restrictions on new build, and in Germany where social housing provided by private landlords passes to the market rental sector once subsidised loans have been repaid. The policy-driven nature of social housing is illustrated by the recent reversal in the long-term decline in the social housing stock in England, due to an increase in building and a tightening of the terms of the Right to Buy scheme.

Elsewhere, the sector has more or less held its own, with small proportionate declines being the most common trend. This undermines the notion that there is a significant downward trajectory in the demand for social rented housing. Indeed, a survey of 12 advanced economies found that in every country not only did the demand for social rented housing greatly exceed its supply, but the demand reflected an underlying need (in the sense that there was evidence of significant numbers of people being unable to access affordable housing of an acceptable quality through the market, but they could not access social rented housing) (Fitzpatrick and Stephens 2007).

Yet, despite its decline, England retains one of the largest social rented sectors in the world (see Figure 2, below).

Figure 2: The size of the social rented sector

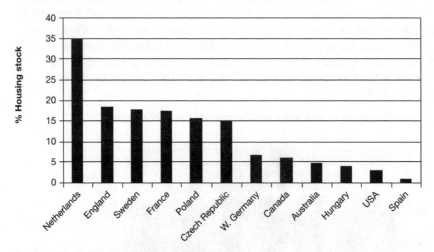

Source: Fitzpatrick and Stephens (2007, Figure 2.1).

This has a bearing on the balance between the other roles that the social rented sector plays in the sphere of consumption (see Figure 3, opposite).

Figure 3: Dominant roles of the social rented sector

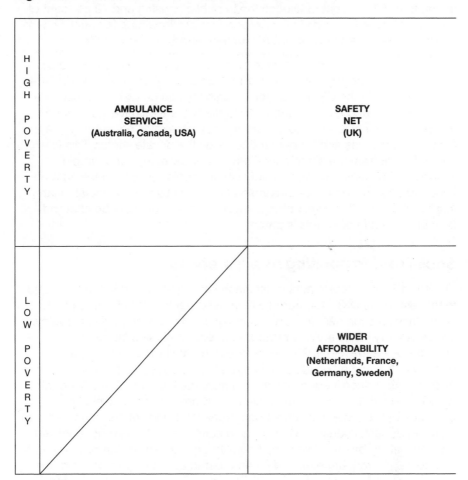

H I G H **P O V E R T Y**	**AMBULANCE SERVICE** (Australia, Canada, USA)

In the diagram:

HIGH POVERTY — **AMBULANCE SERVICE** (Australia, Canada, USA) | **SAFETY NET** (UK)

LOW POVERTY — | **WIDER AFFORDABILITY** (Netherlands, France, Germany, Sweden)

Social rented housing as an 'ambulance service'

In the 'English-speaking' countries of the United States, Canada and Australia, social rented housing never played the supply role to anything like the extent that it did in Europe, and this is reflected in the very small scale of the sector in these countries. When the small scale of the social rented sector is combined with the relatively high levels of poverty and inequality, and the generally weak social security system, as is most clearly seen in the United States, an explanation can be found as to why the social rented sector can be characterised as performing an 'ambulance service' function.

This term is chosen to reflect the way in which eligibility is usually very tightly prescribed in terms of income but, increasingly, access is granted only to those who have an additional vulnerability, such as a disability or other support need. In Canada, for example, special needs allocations account for 58 per cent of allocations to public housing and 70 per cent of community housing, and similar proportions of allocations to special needs groups are reported in Australia (Fitzpatrick and Stephens 2007).

The notion of social rented housing as being an ambulance service also captures its temporary nature. Once the 'emergency' is over, eligibility may be withdrawn. In the US and Canada, eligibility can be lost once incomes rise above the income limit; and in Australia two states have introduced fixed-term tenancies with the possibility that, on expiry, households may lose their tenancies and be directed towards the private sector. This is very different from the situation in France and Germany, for example, where maximum income limits apply when people apply for housing, but if incomes rise above these thresholds once they become a social tenant, eligibility is not withdrawn: rather a supplementary rent may be charged (and implementation of this is patchy).

Social rented housing as a 'safety net'

The social rented sector acts most clearly as a 'safety net' in England (and in the rest of the UK). Compared with most other Western European and Scandinavian countries, the UK has a high level of poverty and inequality. These poverty levels may be attributed to economic and labour market changes since the mid-1970s, when the trend towards greater equality was reversed, and a social security system that does less than elsewhere in Europe to reduce inequalities arising from the labour market. Although working-age, out-of-work benefits in the UK are set at low levels, the coverage of the system is almost comprehensive and, when combined with Housing Benefit, is designed to act as a safety net that prevents post-rent incomes falling below a basic minimum income (see also Kemp, Chapter 4). Of course, in-work benefits and means-tested assistance for low-income pensioners and for households with children have become much more generous through the tax credit system introduced by Gordon Brown.

Eligibility for social rented housing in England is broadly drawn and, very unusually, there is no income limit on eligibility. From the 1970s onwards, allocations systems placed more emphasis on prioritising households that are in the greatest housing need. The homelessness legislation first introduced in 1977 reinforced this trend, and the Homelessness Act 2002 took things a stage further by removing the power of local authorities to introduce blanket exclusions on certain categories of applicant (for example, on grounds of age). As in other countries, certain restrictions have been introduced that relate largely to behaviour, such as antisocial behaviour, although the threshold is set quite high (Fitzpatrick and Stephens 2007). While there is no income limit on eligibility to social rented housing, allocations based on need tend to correlate to targeting housing on those applicants with low incomes.

It is not just new tenants who are poor: many better-off tenants left the sector after 1980 by exercising the right to buy, while those that remained were likely to be exposed to the effects of economical restructuring that accelerated from the mid-1970s and through the 1980s. While unemployment has fallen to levels not seen since the mid-1970s, there has been a growth in working-age households with no one in work, and these are over-represented in the social rented sector.

A previous analysis (Stephens et al 2002) characterised the allocation of social rented housing in the UK as being like 'a strictly means-tested benefit' (p.7) because, once the size of the sector was taken into account, the lowest income deciles were greatly over-represented in the British social rented sector compared to those in Germany and the Netherlands (where its distribution was more akin to a less severely means-tested benefit) and France (where its distribution was likened to a flat-rate benefit with a high cut-off point). The graphs are not reproduced here because the data is now rather dated, but a graph with recent data comparing the Netherlands and England illustrates the point vividly (see Figure 4, below).

Figure 4: Representation of income deciles in social rented housing

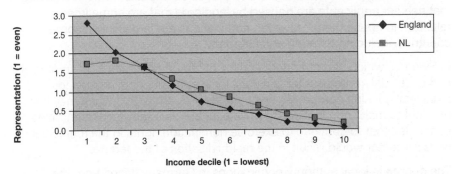

Source: English House Condition Survey, WoonOnderzoek Nederland.

Social rented housing and the 'wider affordability function'

The Scandinavian countries – and also the Netherlands – have much lower levels of poverty and inequality than the UK. France and Germany also have somewhat lower levels of poverty and inequality. These differences arise, in part, from the operation of the labour market, and also from social security systems that place a much greater emphasis on contributory social insurance benefits which generally lead to higher levels of benefits for households, especially those not in the labour market. Particularly when combined with significant social rented sectors, these allow the social rented sector to play a role that can be characterised as a 'wider affordability function'.

Eligibility for social rented housing in Western Europe and Scandinavia is certainly much wider than in the United States and Canada. While Sweden is the only one among these countries that applies no income limit, these are generally drawn sufficiently broadly to permit allocations some way up the income scale. For example, in Germany almost 40 per cent of households are eligible, and in the Netherlands, where 35 per cent of households live in the social rented sector, eligibility cannot be too tightly prescribed.

Allocations systems attempt to balance the provision of housing for people in housing need with a desire to promote the wider affordability function, but there is nonetheless a tendency for the poorer or most vulnerable groups to be excluded from the mainstream tenure.

The Dutch choice-based lettings system illustrates this point. While chronology (time waited) is the principal 'currency' in the system that allows applicants to 'bid' for preferred properties, a 'priority card' is available for the neediest groups to gain faster access. However, access under the priority card is often restricted to parts of the stock that are of a lower quality and cheaper than the rest of it.

Local authority nominations have also played an important role in ensuring that needier applicants are housed by landlords that are sometimes reluctant to house them. However, nominations are in decline in some countries, including Sweden and Germany.

In Sweden, which had operated a policy of tenure neutrality (and so officially had no 'social' rented sector as such), local authority nominations to municipal housing companies went into decline after 1993 when they lost the right to make nominations to private landlords. Many local authorities concluded that to continue to exercise nomination rights in the municipal housing sector would result in the residualisation of the tenure.

The decline in local authority nominations in Germany arises from the shrinkage of the social rented sector – caused in part by the 'natural' shrinkage of the sector as social housing provided by private landlords enters the market rental sector once subsidised loans are repaid. More recently, the decline in nominations has been exacerbated by the tendency for some local authorities (notably Dresden) to sell off their municipal housing company stocks to private landlords (often in the form of private equity companies).

Even where nomination systems remain in place, their effectiveness in securing social housing for poorer and more vulnerable households can be undermined by landlords that are unwilling to house them. In France, nominations do not have to be justified and, so long as they take their quota, landlords are able to decline to house those people they do not wish to have as tenants.

It is important to recognise that the greater 'income mixing' that is often regarded as being far superior to the UK system is achieved, in part, by the explicit exclusion of poorer and vulnerable households from the mainstream social rented sector.

We have already seen how households using the 'priority card' within the Dutch system are often directed to cheaper housing within the social rented sector. In France and Sweden, distinct sub-sectors exist within the social rented sector. The French 'very social' sector was established in 1990 to house people on very low incomes or who have difficulty in integrating into society. It has lower rents than the mainstream social sector and also a lower income limit, although security of tenure may also be weaker. It represents 2.5 per cent of the total social sector.

In Sweden, local authorities run a 'secondary' housing market for households that the municipal housing companies are reluctant to house. The properties are sub-let by the local authority to the tenant, there is no security of tenure and additional conditions may be attached to the tenancy. These may include an obligation to desist from certain kinds of behaviour (eg, smoking or drinking in the flat), to complete certain programmes, or to permit access to social workers.

Inter- and intra-tenure polarisation

There is an inescapable trade-off between balancing the different roles of social housing. Clearly, it is more acute where the levels of poverty are higher and the size of the social rented sector is smaller. Yet it is important to recognise that, even where the trade-off occurs in relatively benign circumstances (for example, Denmark and Sweden) where the levels of poverty are comparatively low and significant social rented sectors exist, there is nonetheless a tendency for populations to become segregated.

This may be explained by contrasting inter-tenure polarisation (ie polarisation between tenures leading to a concentration of poor households in the social rented sector) with intra-tenure polarisation (polarisation *within* tenure). Countries that have lower levels of inter-tenure polarisation than England may nonetheless experience intra-tenure polarisation. Both result in spatial polarisation.

For example, in Denmark and Sweden there is a tendency for poorer tenants to be housed in newer, but less popular, social rented estates on the periphery of cities, while better-off tenants occupy older, but more popular, stock in the central areas (Stephens et al 2002). This finding is supported by a recent overview of the Nordic countries which confirmed that:

'[T]he Nordic countries *share* the *tendencies* for *negative development spirals* to emerge in large suburban developments from the 1960s and 1970s that are characterised by large, uniform and monotonous buildings, building damage and physical deterioration, high tenant turn-over, departure of advantaged residents, etc.' (Hamburger 2004, p.235, italics in original).

These 'tendencies' have been attributed to changes in the labour market, family structures and the operation of the housing market itself (ibid).

Implications for English housing policy

While the 'safety net' function of the English social rented sector is one that appears, on some criteria at least, to produce 'good' housing outcomes for low-income households (see Chapter 1), it is also one that leads to concerns about the concentrations of poverty within it. In particular, the concentration of workless households in the social rented sector is a striking feature of the sector that was highlighted by the evaluation of English housing policy conducted for the Government (by Stephens et al 2005) and the Hills review (Hills 2007), and which is examined further in this volume by Robinson (Chapter 7).

Recently, the issue of worklessness among social tenants has been taken up by the Housing Minister (Flint 2008). In her speech to a Fabian Society conference she acknowledged positive attributes of social rented housing, but located these in the past, 'it isn't so many years ago that a council house was something to prize,' and '[o]riginally, council housing brought together people from different social backgrounds and professions but this has declined'.

At the time of the speech, the most attention was placed on the idea of attaching conditions to social tenancies in order to encourage new tenants to improve their employability. Yet it is revealing that each time the possibility of finding employment is raised, it is assumed that the tenant would then wish to become an owner-occupier, '[b]y helping people into work and onto the property ladder,' and '... there are many [social tenants] who are currently unemployed who could find work with the right training and support. Many social tenants have a real appetite for change and self-improvement. Most say they'd like to own their own home.' (Ibid.)

This approach suggests that the desired policy outcome is to shift the emphasis of England's social rented sector from that of 'safety net' to the position of 'ambulance service'. The 'pathway' for a workless tenant appears to be training and support that will lead to a job which, in turn, will enable them to become a homeowner. It seems likely that the jobs that currently workless tenants will gain are unlikely to permit them to access home ownership on the open market, which in turn implies some form of assisted ownership through the Right to Buy scheme or some form of shared ownership. If this leads to the tenant leaving the area, then the problem of spatial polarisation will be perpetuated; if it is achieved in situ then the stock of available social rented housing will shrink, in time nudging the sector further towards the 'ambulance role'.

Neither of these seems to be desirable outcomes and both are avoidable. If the 'right training and support' can succeed in creating employment among workless social tenants, there is no necessity to subsidise them in order to become homeowners. Moreover, if there are indeed area effects (see Kintrea, Chapter 5), then any substantial rise in working residents would be beneficial for the area as a whole.

Conclusion

In this chapter it has been argued that social rented housing in England (and the rest of the UK) plays a distinctive role in that it provides a 'safety net' for a substantial proportion of low-income households. Its relatively large size enables it to do this, in contrast to some English-speaking countries, notably the United States, where it performs the role of an 'ambulance service' for very low-income households, often with additional support needs.

The relatively high level of poverty in England prevents the social rented sector from playing more of an 'affordability' function for a wider range of households, as it does in several Western European and Scandinavian countries. Although it should be noted that many of these latter countries also exclude the poorest and most vulnerable households from the mainstream social rented sector.

There has been a long-standing concern about the way in which tenure polarisation in England also results in the concentration of low-income tenants in particular neighbourhoods (see Chapter 5). More recently, the concern has become focused on the high level of worklessness among tenants of social landlords.

This chapter makes no judgement on whether there is a causal link between tenure and (lack of) employment; nor does it comment on the suggestion that social tenancies should become conditional on pursuing a programme that is designed to lead to employment (but see Robinson, Chapter 7).

However, it does question the automatic link that has been made between a tenant gaining employment and them becoming a homeowner. There seems to be a curious contradiction in this position whereby the high level of worklessness among social tenants is decried, yet should a social tenant find employment it seems that they are expected to move on to another tenure.

At the very best, the arguments that have been advanced in favour of changing the rights and responsibilities of social tenants conflate a number of arguments and issues. Much clearer thinking is needed if we are to have a worthwhile debate about the 'role of social housing in the twenty-first century'.

Mark Stephens is Professor of European Housing and Assistant Director of the Centre for Housing Policy, University of York.

References

CLG, 2007. *Homes for the future: more affordable, more sustainable.* (The Housing Green Paper) (Cmnd.7191) London: CLG. Available at: http://tinyurl.com/5ku5wu

DETR and DSS, 2000. *Quality and choice: a decent home for all.* (The Housing Green Paper) London: DETR and DSS.

Elsinga, M. and Wassenberg, F., 2007. Social housing in the Netherlands. In C. Whitehead and K. Scanlon. *Social housing in Europe.* London: LSE, p. 130–147.

Fitzpatrick, S. and Stephens, M., 2007. *An international review of homelessness and social housing policy.* London: DCLG. Available at: http://tinyurl.com/59hcfk

Flint, C., 2008. 'Address to the Fabian Society', *Future of Housing* conference, London, 5 Feb. Available at: http://tinyurl.com/5m7vaf

Hamburger, C., 2004. Links between housing policy, social policy and urban policy. In M. Lujanen, ed. *Housing and housing policy in the Nordic Countries.* Copenhagen: Nordic Council of Ministers, p.223–242.

Hills, J., 2007. *Ends and means: the future roles of social housing in England.* CASE Report 34. London: CASE and LSE. Available at: http://tinyurl.com/24ms5b

Levy-Vroelant, C. and Tutin, C., 2007. Social housing in France. In C. Whitehead and K. Scanlon. *Social housing in Europe.* London: LSE, p.70–89.

ODPM, 2005. *Sustainable communities: homes for all. A five-year plan from the Office of the Deputy Prime Minister.* (Cm 6424) Norwich: HMSO.

Stephens, M., Burns, N. and McKay, L., 2002. *Social market or safety net? British social rented housing in a European context.* Bristol: Policy Press.

Stephens, M., Whitehead, C. and Munro, M., 2005. *Lessons from the past, challenges for the future for housing policy: an evaluation of English housing policy 1975–2000.* London: ODPM. Available at: http://tinyurl.com/645au3

Whitehead, C., 2007. Social housing in England. In C. Whitehead and K. Scanlon. *Social housing in Europe.* London: LSE, p. 54–69.

Chapter 3

The contribution of the statutory homelessness system

Suzanne Fitzpatrick

Introduction

This chapter seeks to establish that the statutory homelessness system is an important element of the 'housing settlement' that facilitates relatively good outcomes for poorer households in England as compared with their counterparts elsewhere in Europe. While the homelessness legislation impacts directly on a relatively small number of households on an annual basis, all are poor and assessed as in acute housing need, and the legislation, it is argued, forms a key element of the safety net available to them.

The first section of the chapter briefly outlines the history of the homelessness legislation in England and the wider UK, and places this legislation in an international context to demonstrate its uniqueness. The second section of the chapter outlines the evidence available on the impacts of the statutory homelessness system, drawing heavily on a recently published large-scale study of statutorily homeless families and young people in England. The third section of this chapter is more evaluative, reflecting on whether a 'rights-based' approach is the best way to achieve positive outcomes for homeless households. The fourth and final section considers the implications of recent developments with respect to the statutory homelessness framework, particularly the current emphasis on homelessness prevention and housing options approaches.

A unique safety net?

The British welfare state's first statutory response to homelessness was contained in the National Assistance Act 1948 (Robson and Poustie 1996). This Act placed a duty on local authority welfare departments to provide temporary accommodation for persons in 'urgent need thereof' whose homelessness 'could not reasonably have been foreseen'. Many welfare departments interpreted their obligation to apply exclusively to mothers and children of homeless families, meaning that homeless fathers were frequently excluded from temporary accommodation, and single homeless people were rarely given any assistance at all. Political pressure mounted for intervention from central Government, following the broadcast of the TV drama *Cathy come home* in 1966 and the establishment of Shelter around the same time (Somerville 1999). This eventually resulted in the Housing (Homeless Persons) Act 1977, which originated as a Private Members Bill but was assisted by the then Labour Government in its route through Parliament.

The overall goals of the 1977 Act were to provide *long-term* housing solutions[1] for homeless households, especially families with children and vulnerable single adults, and to transfer responsibilities for these households from local authority social services to housing departments (Fitzpatrick and Stephens 1999). The original Act applied to England, Scotland and Wales, with the legislation extended to Northern Ireland in 1988.

There have been a series of minor and more significant amendments made to the statutory homelessness framework since it came into force in 1978, and this complex history is discussed in detail elsewhere (Fitzpatrick 2005). This chapter will focus on the statutory framework as it currently stands in England.[2] This provides that eligible[3] applicants found to be homeless[4], in priority need[5], and unintentionally homeless[6] must be accommodated (together with their household) by the local authority to which they apply as homeless.[7] Strictly speaking, this 'main homelessness duty' is to secure temporary accommodation until suitable settled housing becomes available, found either by the household itself or by the local authority. (In keeping with the common convention, the term 'statutorily homeless' is used in this chapter to denote those households who are accepted as

---

[1] As subsequent legal and policy developments have generated controversy over this point, it is worth referring to the original House of Commons Debate which makes clear that both those supporting and those opposing the Bill assumed that the great majority of qualifying households would be rehoused in permanent council tenancies (House of Commons Debate; HC Deb.) (1977) Housing (Homeless Persons) Bill, Second Reading, c.905, 18 February.

[2] Contained in Part 7 of the Housing Act 1996, as amended by the Homelessness Act 2002 and associated secondary legislation.

[3] Certain categories of 'persons from abroad', including asylum seekers, are 'ineligible' for assistance under the homelessness legislation.

[4] The statutory definition of 'homelessness' comprises persons without any accommodation in the UK that they have a legal right to occupy, together with their whole household. It also includes those who cannot gain access to their accommodation, or cannot reasonably be expected to live in it (for example, because of a risk of violence.) By international standards, this is a very wide definition of homelessness (Fitzpatrick and Stephens 2007).

[5] The 'priority need' groups comprise persons whose household contains: a dependent child; a pregnant woman; a young person aged 16 or 17 (or 18–20 years old if formerly in local authority care); any person who has lost her/his accommodation as a result of an emergency, such as flood, fire or other disaster; or someone who is vulnerable because of a particular reason, such as age, disability, fleeing violence, or an institutional background.

[6] They have not brought about their homelessness by their own deliberate actions or inaction.

[7] The only exception to this is if the applicant's household has no 'local connection' with the local authority to which they apply and does have a local connection with another British local authority, then, subject to certain conditions (eg, no risk of violence in the relevant area), responsibility can be transferred to the latter local authority.

owed the main homelessness duty under the homelessness legislation.)
However, in practice, settled housing is almost always secured by the local
authority that owes a duty under the homelessness legislation. In the great
majority of cases, discharge of the local authority duty is through the offer
of a social rented tenancy, with security of tenure (Pleace et al 2008).[8] It is
also possible for a local authority to discharge its duty through the offer of
a fixed-term tenancy (an assured shorthold tenancy) in the private rented
sector. At present, this requires the explicit consent of the applicant, but
there have been hints that the Government may consider legislating to allow
for compulsory discharge of duty into fixed-term private sector tenancies
(Office of the Deputy Prime Minister (ODPM) 2005).[9]

While the relevant legal provisions are expressed as duties on the local
authority, rather than as rights for homeless persons, from the outset the
courts have held that these obligations are clear and specific enough for
homeless applicants to have title and interest to challenge decisions under
this legislation through judicial review. Homeless applicants are now entitled
to an internal review of most aspects of the decision on their application,
and a statutory appeal to the county court on a point of law is also provided.

Such enforceable rights – ie rights which a court of law will enforce on
behalf of individuals – appear to be highly unusual in the homelessness
field. In a recent review of homelessness and social housing policy in 12
developed economies, England was unique in having enforceable rights for
(some) homeless people, the ultimate discharge of which involved making
available *settled housing* (Fitzpatrick and Stephens 2007). In several other
European countries there is a right to housing contained in the national
constitution, but no legal mechanisms are provided to enable homeless
individuals to enforce these rights. With regards to Sweden, for example:

> 'The constitution… includes the word "right" but this was never
> interpreted to mean that there was an enforceable right to housing for
> the individual citizen.' (Sahlin 2005, p.15.)

In France, a vociferous protest campaign resulted in emergency legislation
being passed in 2007 which aims to establish a legally-enforceable right to
housing. Thus, from January 2012, all social housing applicants who have
experienced 'an abnormally long delay' in being allocated accommodation
can apply to an administrative tribunal to demand that the state provides
them with housing. Certain priority categories, including homeless people,
will benefit from this legislation from December 2008. However, this
legislation was passed very quickly in response to media pressure, and
there are concerns that the complexities of the politico-administrative

---

[8] Although social landlords may issue introductory tenancies ('probationary tenancies') to new
tenants, usually lasting one year. These tenancies normally convert to standard secure tenancies
at the end of this period.

[9] There are also a number of other circumstances that bring the duty to an end, such as where
the household voluntarily leaves the temporary accommodation provided by the local authority.

framework in France will frustrate its implementation (Loison 2008). It is certainly far removed from the Scottish model – whereby virtually all homeless people will have a right to permanent rehousing by 2012 (Anderson 2008) – which some commentators in France had hoped it would emulate.

Figure 1: Enforceable rights to accommodation

	Rights requiring settled housing to be made available to homeless people	Rights to emergency accommodation for homeless people
Australia	No	No
Canada	No	No
US	No	Only in New York City – for roofless people
Germany	No	Yes – for roofless people
France	Yes – from December 2008, for homeless people (alongside other priority groups) who have experienced an abnormally long delay in being allocated social housing. But serious doubts remain over implementation	No
Netherlands	No	No
Sweden	No	Yes – for roofless people
Spain	No	No
England	Yes – for those who are eligible, in a priority need group, and not intentionally homeless	Yes – if they are eligible and in a priority need group (being roofless is neither necessary nor sufficient)
Czech Republic	No	No
Hungary	No	Yes – for roofless people
Poland	No	Yes – for roofless people

Source: Fitzpatrick and Stephens (2007).

As Figure 1, above, demonstrates, while enforceable rights linked to the provision of settled housing were limited to England and France (with serious doubts about the practical implementation of such rights in the latter), Fitzpatrick and Stephens (2007) found that there were enforceable rights to *emergency accommodation* in a number of the other surveyed countries. For example, in Germany, municipalities have a legally-enforceable obligation under police laws to accommodate homeless persons who would otherwise be roofless. Similarly, in Sweden, social services legislation obliges municipalities to ensure that nobody within their territory 'suffers' – this is interpreted to include an entitlement to emergency accommodation. In Poland, social welfare law requires communes to offer help to homeless people, including shelter in hostels, refuges and other institutional settings. In Hungary, local municipalities are obliged to provide accommodation in shelters for people whose 'physical well-being is at risk'. A single jurisdiction within the US – New York City – provides a legally-enforceable right to accommodation for the 'truly homeless' who have absolutely nowhere else to go.

In all of these cases it is notable that the entitlement falls far short of the right to temporary accommodation until suitable settled accommodation becomes available, which applies in England for statutorily homeless households. On the other hand, it is worth noting from Figure 1 that there are no legal rights to emergency accommodation for roofless people in England unless they are in a priority need group and are eligible for assistance. In this sense the *legal* safety net in England is weaker than in the countries just discussed, although it should be acknowledged that government-funded programmes have provided considerable assistance to rough sleepers in recent years (Randall and Brown 2002).

The impacts of the statutory homelessness system

So far, we have established that the statutory homelessness system in England and the wider UK is a highly unusual, and probably unique, legal framework. However, that uniqueness does not, in and of itself, establish that it is a 'good thing' that ought to be preserved. Until recently, there has been little evidence available on the impacts and outcomes of the homelessness system, from the perspective of those who have experienced it.[10] However, a nationally representative study of the experiences of families with children and 16–17 year olds accepted by their local authority as being owed the main homelessness duty has recently been published (Pleace et al 2008), providing the most comprehensive insight into the role of the statutory system to date.

Perhaps the most significant finding of this study was that the provision of assistance under the homelessness legislation appeared to have secured a substantial net improvement in the quality of life of both families and young people. Thus, those parents who reported that life was now better than in their last settled accommodation[11] heavily outnumbered those for whom it was perceived to be worse (57 per cent as compared with 19 per cent). Likewise, they were far more likely to report an improvement (57 per cent) than a decline (12 per cent) in their child(ren)'s overall quality of life. The reported net improvement in overall quality of life since last settled accommodation was greatest for those families living in settled housing by point of interview[12], but there was nonetheless a substantial net improvement for those still in temporary accommodation. Young people were also much more likely to say that life was better (52 per cent),

---

[10] Previous major studies, such as O'Callaghan et al (1996), focused on the processes associated with the homelessness legislation and its housing outcomes, rather than on its broader impact on homeless households' wellbeing.

[11] Parents were asked about a range of their family's circumstances in their 'last settled accommodation' prior to acceptance as homeless, as a means of investigating whether there was evidence of changes that could be associated with the experience of statutory homelessness and temporary accommodation.

[12] By the time of interview, on average, nine months after acceptance as homeless, 55 per cent of families, most of them in the North and Midlands, had been rehoused into settled accommodation (almost always social rented housing). The remaining 45 per cent, mainly in London and the South, were still in temporary accommodation (usually self-contained temporary accommodation, much of it leased from the private rented sector).

rather than worse (25 per cent), than it had been in their last settled accommodation, although for this group there was no association with whether they were in settled or temporary housing.[13]

Despite concerns expressed in previous research, the net impacts of homelessness and spending time in temporary accommodation on the health and social support circumstances of parents in these families appeared to be largely negligible, or even marginally positive. Moreover, some positive net changes were reported for children since leaving their last settled accommodation, particularly with regards to their school performance and their relationship with their parents. However, some negative net changes were also apparent for children in relation to loneliness and reduced participation in clubs/activities. One-third of school-aged children had changed school as a direct result of homelessness, and, perhaps surprisingly, this could have powerful negative or positive effects on outcomes for these children. With respect to young people, statutory homelessness had little net effect on their self-reported health status, and their access to social support had actually improved overall since they left their last settled accommodation, primarily because of increased access to professional sources of support.

In contrast to these generally positive, or at least mixed, findings with regards to the social impacts of statutory homelessness, there was a clearly negative 'economic' effect. Families reported a net increase of 15 percentage points in levels of worklessness since leaving their last settled accommodation (64 per cent of families were workless at point of interview).[14] Almost one-half (47 per cent) of families reported that they were now finding it more difficult to manage financially than in their last settled accommodation, with only 18 per cent saying that their financial situation had improved. Even worse economic impacts were reported by young people: approximately one-third (34 per cent) of young people had discontinued participation in the education system, employment or training since leaving their last settled accommodation, offset to only a very small degree by the four per cent who had taken up one of these activities. Echoing the findings on families, 56 per cent of young people reported that their ability to manage financially had declined since leaving their last settled accommodation, and only 12 per cent said that it had improved.

It was noted above that those in settled (almost always social) housing were most likely to report an *improvement* in their overall quality of life since leaving their last settled accommodation. They also reported a far better *current*

---

[13] At point of survey, on average, nine months after acceptance as homeless, 40 per cent of young people had moved into settled housing, and 60 per cent were still living in temporary accommodation.

[14] This was not explained by relationship breakdown and the departure of a working adult from the household. It should also be noted that, as this was not a longitudinal study, we don't know if this rise in worklessness is sustained in the long term, or is instead a temporary consequence of the disruption associated with homelessness.

quality of life than those still living in temporary accommodation. In particular, while the majority of parents in temporary accommodation considered their lives to be 'on hold' (64 per cent), this was true of only 18 per cent of those in settled housing. Parents in temporary accommodation were also more likely than those in settled housing to worry about the future and to report lower levels of overall happiness.[15] Among children, only 34 per cent of those in temporary accommodation, as compared with 52 per cent of those in settled housing, reported being 'very happy'. Moreover, and despite mixed results with regards to the relative physical standards in settled and temporary accommodation, both parents and children reported markedly higher levels of satisfaction with settled housing than with self-contained (or indeed any other form of) temporary accommodation. These findings suggest that the security of tenure offered by settled (social) housing is very important to both parents and children in families accepted as homeless.

Young people living in temporary accommodation were much more likely than those in settled housing to perceive their life to be 'on hold' (57 per cent as compared with 18 per cent, respectively). However, in contrast to parents in homeless families, neither worrying about the future nor general levels of (un)happiness were associated with living in temporary accommodation. Moreover, young people in settled housing were only marginally more satisfied with their accommodation than those still in temporary accommodation. Thus, for young people accepted as homeless 16–17 years olds, it appears that security of tenure is a less pressing concern at this very early stage in their housing career than it is for families with children.[16]

Evaluating the homelessness legislation

The findings of Pleace et al (2008) can, to a large extent, be viewed as a 'good news story' with regards to the impacts associated with the statutory homelessness system. However, arguments in favour of the homelessness legislation cannot rely solely on demonstrably positive outcomes for households who have experienced the statutory system. For one thing, it remains debatable whether the rights-based approach encapsulated in the statutory homelessness framework is the only, or best, way to achieve positive outcomes for homeless households. For example, in Ireland, good progress on addressing homelessness is said to have been made despite an explicit rejection of a rights-based approach (which they view as 'ideological') in favour of a consensus-based 'social partnership' model.[17]

---

[15] All of these outcomes were subjected to multi-variable analysis which established that there was a significant independent effect of living in temporary or settled accommodation once a range of demographic, geographical, and personal variables, as well physical accommodation conditions, were taken into account.

[16] This remark refers specifically to 16–17 year olds accepted as homeless. It should not be taken to imply that older young people aged up to 25, particularly those with family responsibilities, do not value security of tenure.

[17] Personal correspondence with Dr Eoin O'Sullivan, Lecturer in Social Policy, Trinity College, Dublin. See also Bengtsson (2001).

Key to the Irish position seems to be the idea that right-based frameworks encourage a legalistic/rationing emphasis rather than a problem-solving/ flexible approach. However, while it should be conceded that an adversarial emphasis is a real, and to some extent inevitable, hazard of the rights-based approach, this drawback has to be weighed against the considerable empowerment that may be afforded to homeless people by enforceable legal rights, especially where these rights are allied to effective advocacy services. For this reason the European Federation of Organisations Working with the Homeless (FEANTSA) has, for many years, been advocating a rights-based approach to addressing homelessness across the EU.[18] It is also worth mentioning in this context the *Loi Besson*[19] in France, passed in 1990 and lauded at the time as a 'programmatic' rather than 'individualistic' attempt to realise a right to housing by tying it to a package of local planning and finance (Harvey 1994). This *Loi* might, as in the Irish case, be considered to encapsulate a consensus, or partnership, approach, but has clearly been adjudged deficient as a means of ensuring homeless people's access to housing, hence the attempt to switch to an enforceable rights-based approach, as noted above.

A different ground of objection to the homelessness legislation, and the associated 'reasonable preference' criterion in local authority housing allocations, concerns the degree to which it can actually be credited with improving long-term housing outcomes for homeless families (ie would the same people have been housed anyway without the 1977 Act?). The Audit Commission (1989, p.19) found that the housing officers interviewed during their study believed that:

> '... the great majority of homeless households currently being accepted for housing in their authority were people to whom the council would in any event have given priority.'

While we are not able to test this counterfactual assertion with any degree of rigour, policy analysis has suggested that the additional benefit accruing to statutorily homeless households was significant (Fitzpatrick 2005), particularly as the legislation appears to have encouraged a change in attitude towards homeless households at local authority level (Robson and Poustie 1996). It was certainly a key component in the overall shift away from housing allocations systems dominated by merit, towards those based on need (Fitzpatrick and Stephens 1999). Moreover, international evidence provides strong grounds for thinking that a key benefit of the homeless persons legislation is that it makes it far more difficult for social landlords to exclude the poorest and most vulnerable households from the

---

[18] And the strongly rights-based 'Scottish model' has attracted significant attention from homelessness advocates throughout Europe and beyond (Anderson 2008).

[19] Loi Besson is the common name for the French Housing Act 1990. This Act provides that all local authorities should ensure that at least 20 per cent of housing in their area is social rented.

mainstream social rented sector, as happens in a number of other European countries (see Stephens, Chapter 2). Of course, in addition to any benefits with regards to permanent housing, the statutory framework also provides a 'safety net' of temporary accommodation for qualifying households that would not otherwise exist.

Whatever its merits, problems clearly remain with the statutory homelessness system. First, there is its limited coverage: as noted above, even roofless people, unless they have a priority need, have no legal entitlement to emergency accommodation in England. This narrowness of coverage is related to the extent of assistance offered – more limited rights, such as access to emergency accommodation, could more readily be offered to all homeless people. The link with settled housing makes extending these rights difficult in England[20], especially in high demand areas such as London. In fact, it is arguable whether even current homelessness entitlements are deliverable in the exceptionally tight housing market conditions of London, particularly given the acute shortfall in social rented housing in the capital (see Bramley, Chapter 8; Monk et al, Chapter 9). Stays in temporary accommodation can be extremely lengthy in London, leading to high levels of frustration among statutorily homeless households (Pleace et al 2008), and huge demands on the public purse. Moreover, and despite its high cost, physical conditions are often reported to be poor within temporary accommodation in London and elsewhere in the South of England.

Hills (2007, p.166) highlighted another longstanding concern with the statutory framework, which is the perception that it creates a perverse incentive to take the 'homelessness route' as a 'fast-track' to a social tenancy. However, it is important to bear in mind here that statutorily homeless households are not entitled to overriding priority but rather to 'reasonable preference' in housing allocations; not only do many spend lengthy periods in temporary accommodation before being allocated a social tenancy, they are often disadvantaged with respect to the degree of choice they exercise over the allocations they eventually receive (see Pawson, Chapter 6). Moreover, it appears from Pleace et al (2008) that such perverse incentives as exist within the homelessness legislation are extremely muted in their practical effects. Thus, only very small numbers of statutorily homeless families and young people reported that they had applied as homeless because they perceived this to be the quickest or only way to gain access to social housing (between three and six per cent). The great majority (85 per cent) of both families and young people had made efforts to gain alternative help with their housing problems before approaching the council for assistance.

However, even in the absence of any major anxieties with respect to perverse incentives, there remains the concern that lettings to statutory

---

[20] Although in Scotland, as noted above, the very ambitious target has been set of extending entitlement to permanent rehousing to virtually all homeless households by 2012 (Anderson 2008).

homeless households may 'crowd out' lettings to other households in areas of high housing stress. A question mark arises over the fairness of this given that statutory homelessness status can result from a short-term crisis, rather than long-term housing needs that are necessarily any greater than those of other housing applicants (Fitzpatrick and Stephens 1999). Relevant here is Pleace et al's (2008) finding that most statutorily homeless families were not extremely vulnerable, but rather were low-income households who were unable to secure alternative accommodation when confronted with a crisis such as relationship breakdown or eviction which caused them to lose their existing accommodation. In an ideal needs-based system one would perhaps, having dealt with their emergency situation, assess their long-term housing needs on the same basis as those of everyone else seeking social housing (Fitzpatrick and Stephens 1999). Against this, there is the practical imperative associated with the high cost to the public purse of extended stays in temporary accommodation. One might also take the ethical position that the particular distress associated with losing your home in an unplanned way (an especially important issue for children, see Pleace et al 2008), coupled with the insecurity and sense of 'life being on hold' engendered by stays in temporary accommodation, should be given weight in allocations decisions, and the statutory system provides a practicable means for doing so. Thus, I would argue that, taken in the round, the link between statutory homelessness and reasonable priority for long-term housing is justified and should remain.

Perhaps the most important remaining concern about the homelessness legislation is its contribution to the spatial concentration of poor households (see Kintrea, Chapter 5), although again this is partly a function of the quality, as well as quantity, of allocations to this group (Fitzpatrick and Stephens 1999).

The implications of recent developments

The number of households accepted as statutorily homeless fluctuates over time, usually in parallel with trends in housing affordability (Pawson et al 2007). Homelessness acceptances rose steeply in England from the late 1990s, reaching a peak of 135,590 in 2003 (see Figure 2, opposite). The number of statutory homeless households in temporary accommodation awaiting settled housing increased even more rapidly, reaching 101,300 by the end of December 2004. In response to these rising levels of statutory homelessness, particularly in London, there was a step-change in the emphasis placed by central Government on homelessness prevention. The Homelessness Act 2002 introduced a new statutory duty for local authorities to produce a prevention-focused homelessness strategy for their area, and dedicated central government funding was provided to support local prevention activities. An official target was introduced to halve the total number of statutory homeless households in temporary accommodation, from the December 2004 level, by 2010 (ODPM 2005).

As Hills (2007, p.166) has noted, this homelessness prevention strategy has been a 'remarkable success', with an extremely sharp fall in statutory homelessness acceptances since 2003: only 64,970 households were accepted as homeless during 2007, a reduction of 52 per cent in just four years (see Figure 2, below). The number of households in temporary accommodation also fell, albeit more slowly, standing at 79,500 at the end of December 2007.

Figure 2: The number of households accepted as owed the main homelessness duty in England 1997-2007

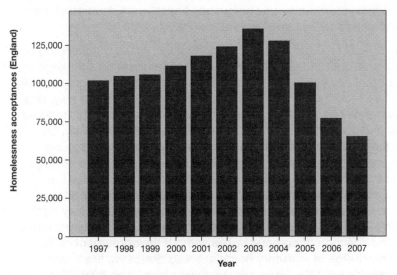

Source: CLG, 2007. Statutory homelessness: 4th quarter 2007, P1E statistics. Available at: http://tinyurl.com/6rqrv5

However, there is considerable controversy over whether these unprecedented post-2003 reductions in statutory homelessness are attributable to the prevention of homelessness or rather to the prevention of homelessness acceptances (Pawson and Davidson 2007). Rashleigh (2005), for example, has argued that, for funding and other reasons, local government staff now feel under acute pressure from central Government to reduce their homelessness acceptance rates. Key here is the 'housing options' approach, strongly promoted by central Government (Department for Communities and Local Government (DCLG) 2006), under which all households approaching a local authority for assistance with housing are given a formal interview offering advice on their housing options, which may include services, such as family mediation or landlord liaison, that are designed to prevent the need to make a homelessness application. The Government's good practice guidance emphasises that housing options interviews should never replace or delay a statutory homelessness application where there is 'reason to believe' that an applicant may be homeless or threatened with homelessness[21], but this is somewhat in tension with its suggestion of a two-stage process 'with options and prevention considered first, but with safeguards in place where a person is eligible for and requires assistance under the homelessness legislation' (DCLG 2006, p.16). O'Hara (2007) has therefore argued that housing options interviews represent a barrier to making an official homelessness application in some areas, and there is evidence that certain local authorities may unlawfully require potential homeless applicants to exhaust all possible preventative avenues before any formal consideration of their statutory homelessness status takes place (Pawson 2007).

Thus, it is difficult to avoid the conclusion that increased gatekeeping on the part of local authorities has contributed to the dramatic shrinkage in statutory homelessness in recent years. However, it seems highly unlikely that the entire recorded reduction can be accounted for in this way, and there is evidence of some creditable successes with respect to targeted homelessness prevention interventions (Pawson et al 2007). Also, the 'culture change' associated with a more pro-active, problem-solving approach under the prevention regime is to be welcomed, addressing as it does the inflexible, legalistic emphasis which can characterise the statutory system. Nonetheless, insofar as the recent sharp drop in homelessness acceptances is attributable to a denial of statutory rights, rather than to genuine prevention, this is a matter for concern. Any future moves in the direction of compulsory (ie without the agreement of the applicant) discharge of statutory homelessness duties via fixed-term private tenancies will also cause great concern insofar as they affect families with children (see above).

Conclusion

This chapter has argued that there are good grounds for concluding that the homelessness legislation in England is a valuable safety net for poor households in acute housing need. The provision of assistance under this statutory framework is associated with substantial net improvements in the quality of life of both families and young people, particularly, in the case of families, once they have been given settled accommodation (almost always in the social rented sector). However, recent developments under the rubric of the 'prevention' agenda, while welcome in many respects, have created scope for legitimate concern that the national, minimum protection offered by the homelessness legislation may progressively be undermined by de facto changes in practice in some areas, even if the de jure position remains unchanged. Far preferable to any 'undermining by stealth' of the legislation, would be an open debate about how to manage the particular difficulties

---

[21] And see Robinson v Hammersmith and Fulham LBC [2006] EWCA Civ 1122.

of delivering on the entitlements of homeless people in London, even if that means consideration of less than ideal measures, such as tightening local connection rules in the capital.

Suzanne Fitzpatrick is Joseph Rowntree Professor of Housing and Director of the Centre for Housing Policy, University of York

References

Anderson, I., 2008. Sustainable solutions to homelessness: the Scottish case. *European Journal of Homelessness,* p.163–183.

Audit Commission, 1989. *Housing the homeless: the local authority role.* London: HMSO.

Bengtsson, B., 2001. Housing as a social right: implications for welfare state theory. *Scandinavian Political Studies,* 24(4), p.255–275.

DCLG, 2006. *Homelessness prevention: a guide to good practice.* London: DCLG.

Fitzpatrick, S., 2005 Statutory homelessness. In M. Stephens, ed. *Evaluation of individual housing policies and technical report, evaluation of English housing policy 1975-2000.* London: ODPM, 2005, p.70–94.

Fitzpatrick, S. and Stephens, M., 1999. Homelessness, need and desert in the allocation of council housing. *Housing Studies,* 14(4), p.413–431.

Fitzpatrick, S. and Stephens, M., 2007. *An international review of homelessness and social housing policy.* London: CLG.

Harvey, B., 1993. Homelessness in Europe – national housing policies and legal rights. *Scandinavian Housing and Planning Research,* 10, p.115–119.

Hills, J., 2007. *Ends and means: the future of social housing in England.* CASE Report 34. London: CASE and LSE. Available at: http://tinyurl.com/24ms5b

Loison, M. The implementation of an enforceable right to housing in France. *European Journal of Homelessness,* 1, p.185–197.

O'Callaghan, B., Dominion, L., Evans, A., Dix, J., Smith, R., Williams, P. and Zimmeck, M., 1996. *Study of homeless applicants.* London: HMSO.

O'Hara, E., 2007. *Rights and wrongs: the homelessness safety net 30 years on.* London: Shelter.

ODPM, 2005. *Sustainable communities: homes for all. A five year plan from the Office of the Deputy Prime Minister.* (Cm. 6424) London: ODPM.

Pawson, H., 2007. Local authority homelessness prevention in England: empowering consumers or denying rights. *Housing Studies,* 22(6), p.867–883.

Pawson, H. and Davidson, E., 2007. Fit for purpose? Official measures of homelessness in the era of the activist. *Radical Statistics,* 93, p.7–29.

Pawson, H., Netto, G., Jones, C., Wager, F., Fancy, C. and Lomax, D., 2007. *Evaluating homelessness prevention.* London: CLG.

Pleace, N., Fitzpatrick, S., Johnsen, S., Quilgars, D. and Sanderson, D., 2008. *Statutory homelessness in England: the experience of families and 16–17 year olds.* London: CLG.

Randall, G. and Brown, S., 2002. *Helping rough sleepers off the streets: a report to the homelessness directorate.* London: ODPM.

Rashleigh, B., 2005. Keeping the numbers down. *ROOF,* January/February.

Robson, P. and Poustie, M., 1996. *Homelessness and the law in Britain.* 3rd ed. London: Butterworths/Planning Exchange.

Sahlin, I., 2005. *Homelessness and the changing role of the state in Sweden.* European Observatory on Homelessness, Thematic Paper, Brussels: FEANTSA.

Somerville, P., 1999. The making and unmaking of the homeless persons legislation. In S. Hutson and D. Clapham, eds. *Homelessness: public policies and private troubles.* London: Cassell.

Chapter 4

Housing Benefit and social housing in England

Peter A Kemp

Introduction

Housing Benefit makes an important contribution to social housing in England. It not only helps the majority of tenants to afford their rent, but also accounts for about half of the rental income of social housing landlords. It is therefore of vital importance for landlords, as well as tenants.[1] Moreover, since approximately £13 billion is paid annually in Housing Benefit to social housing tenants (Hills 2007), the taxpayer also has a considerable financial stake in the scheme.

The significance of Housing Benefit goes well beyond housing. It is an important part of social security provision and interacts with tax credits and the wider income tax system. Furthermore, Housing Benefit can affect work incentives, and hence has potential implications for the prevalence of unemployment and economic inactivity (worklessness) among people of working age. Finally, Housing Benefit redistributes income to the renting poor and thereby helps to reduce income inequality (Gibbs and Kemp 1993).

Housing Benefit is a means-tested social security benefit that is administered by local authorities on behalf of the Department for Work and Pensions (DWP). Unlike many other European countries, mainstream social security benefits in the UK make no provision for the housing costs of people who live in rented accommodation.[2] In consequence, Housing Benefit can cover the whole of the rent in certain circumstances. However, Housing Benefit in the UK goes less far up the income scale than in many other European countries (Kemp 1997).

The structure of this chapter is as follows. It begins with a discussion of the role of Housing Benefit. It then looks at who gets Housing Benefit and its impact on affordability. Next, the chapter considers the relationship between Housing Benefit and incentives to work. It then assesses the potential for extending the Local Housing Allowance to social housing and

---

[1] Housing Benefit is also important for the private rental market, as one in five rent-paying private tenants currently receive this benefit.

[2] However, provision is made in mainstream social security benefits in the UK for mortgage interest payments.

examines the vexed issue of whether Housing Benefit should be paid to the landlord or the tenant. The final section presents some conclusions.

The role of Housing Benefit

Means-tested Housing Benefit schemes can have housing policy or social security objectives. In practice, however, most Housing Benefit schemes in the advanced economies invariably have both functions, though one or the other is usually dominant (Kemp 1997). From a housing policy perspective, the purpose of Housing Benefit is to allow low-income households to afford decent quality housing, ie to raise their level of housing consumption above that which they would otherwise be able to afford.[3] However, from a social security (income support) perspective the role of Housing Benefit is to enable low-income tenants to reduce the share of their income devoted to housing expenditure, ie to reduce their rent to income ratio to an 'affordable' level. By spending less of their income on housing, they can devote more of it to non-housing items in their budget. These two roles – housing consumption and housing affordability – are not necessarily compatible, and can generate conflicting objectives for Housing Benefit between the government departments responsible for housing policy and social security respectively.

Perhaps surprisingly, the role of Housing Benefit has rarely been discussed in depth in official publications. Government statistical publications describe the scheme as being designed to help tenants who 'have difficulty meeting their housing costs' (DWP 2005, p.48), which implies that Housing Benefit primarily performs an income support role. Meanwhile, the 2002 Green Paper on Housing Benefit reform stated that the fundamental purpose of the scheme is 'to ensure that people on low incomes have the opportunity of a decent home' (DWP 2002, p.14), which implies that Housing Benefit is largely an instrument of housing policy.

Housing Benefit is certainly an important part of the social security system. It accounts for a substantial share of the income transfers that are paid to people whose main sources of income are social security benefits and tax credits (Hills 2007). This is particularly true of means-tested social security benefits that are paid to people who are not in work, namely income-based Jobseeker's Allowance, Income Support and the Guarantee Credit Component of Pension Credit.[4] The benefit levels for these income support schemes are based on the assumption that the recipient's rent will be fully covered by Housing Benefit.[5] In other words, Housing Benefit is structured in a way that ensures that recipients of these benefits who are living in social housing have an income after rent is deducted that is equal to the income

---

[3] But not to such a high level that they are deemed to be 'over-consuming' (Stephens 2005).

[4] Hereafter referred to as 'income support benefits' for ease of exposition.

[5] Though non-dependants living with Housing Benefit recipients are expected to contribute to the rent. In these cases, Housing Benefit is reduced by fixed amounts depending on the income of the non-dependant.

support benefit rate. This design suggests that the income support role is more important than the housing one.

Nevertheless, Housing Benefit also plays a critical role in housing policy. It has become an increasingly important part of the housing subsidy system in England. The main cash subsidies that are used to help to make social housing affordable are (i) general subsidies that lower the amount of rent that is charged to all tenants whatever their income or circumstances; and (ii) means-tested Housing Benefit, which targets help on low-income tenants. Since the 1980s, Housing Benefit has become more important, and general subsidies less important, in cash terms. As Figure 1, overleaf, shows, general subsidies have shrunk considerably, especially for housing associations. Housing Benefit now accounts for almost 90 per cent of public expenditure on assistance with housing costs in Britain, and general subsidies for little more than ten per cent.

Housing Benefit is not only important to social housing tenants, but also to their landlords and the financial institutions that lend to them. In 2006/07, an estimated £12.7 billion was paid in Housing Benefit on behalf of social housing tenants in England (Hills 2007). Moreover, it has been estimated that Housing Benefit accounted for 59 per cent of the rental income of local councils and 53 per cent of the rental income of housing associations in England in 2003/04 (Kemp 2007). In effect, Housing Benefit underwrites social housing landlords' rental income stream. It provides them with greater financial security, and potentially enables housing associations to borrow at lower rates of interest than might otherwise be the case. Indeed, the reduction in general subsidies, the increased use of private finance for housing association development activity, and stock transfers from local councils that have taken place since the late 1990s have been predicated on the availability of Housing Benefit to cushion tenants from the consequent rise in rent levels (Stephens 2005).

Figure 1: Cash subsidies in social housing

	1990/91	2005/06
	%	%
Council		
General subsidy	27	3
Means-tested Housing Benefit	73	97
Total	100	100
Housing association		
General subsidy	78	22
Means-tested Housing Benefit	22	78
Total	100	100
All social housing		
General subsidy	41	13
Means-tested Housing Benefit	59	87
Total	100	100

Note: The data are for Great Britain.

Source: calculated from Wilcox, *UK Housing Review 2007/08,* Table 122.

Because of the age of their stock and lack of new construction since the 1970s, many local authority housing revenue accounts are in surplus. This may account for some of the decline in general subsidy for council housing shown in Figure 1, above. Housing revenue accounts are ring-fenced, and surpluses are returned to central Government, which has led to claims that better-off tenants are subsidising the rents of Housing Benefit claimants. The Government has recently announced a review of housing revenue accounts finance, a topic that is beyond the scope of this chapter.

Who receives Housing Benefit?

The *Survey of English Housing* indicates that six out of ten social housing tenants are in receipt of Housing Benefit, a proportion that has been fairly stable over the past decade. In 2005/06, for example, 1,384,000 council tenants (62 per cent of the total) and 972,000 housing association tenants (60 per cent) were on Housing Benefit in England. However, the percentage of social housing tenants receiving Housing Benefit varies by household type. Approximately eight out of ten lone parents with dependent children were on Housing Benefit in 2005/06, which was double the proportion among couples. Seven out of ten single people and approximately six out of ten people living in multi-adult households were also receiving Housing Benefit (see Figure 2, opposite).

Figure 2: Percentage of households in receipt of Housing Benefit, by household type

Household type	Council tenants	Housing association tenants
Couple	47	40
Couple with children*	38	40
Lone parent*	77	81
Multi-person household~	61	57
Single person	72	68

* With dependent children.
~ Multi-person households includes households with only non-dependent children
Source: Survey of English Housing 2005/06.

Not surprisingly, Housing Benefit receipt also varies by economic status (see Figure 3, below). Approximately seven out of ten retired households and nine out of ten unemployed or economically inactive tenants of working age were recipients of Housing Benefit in 2005/06. This compares with roughly one-half of tenants engaged in part-time work and less than one in ten doing full-time work. The 'other economically inactive' group mostly comprises lone parents and people who are long-term sick or disabled.

Figure 3: Percentage of households in receipt of Housing Benefit, by economic status

Economic status*	Council tenants	Housing association tenants
Working full-time	6	8
Working part-time	44	49
Unemployed	86	93
Retired	75	71
Other economically active	88	88

* Economic status of household reference person
Source: Survey of English Housing 2005/06.

The proportion of tenants in receipt of Housing Benefit also varies by income level. This reflects the fact that Housing Benefit is a means-tested scheme. As Figure 4, overleaf, shows, in 2005/06 the proportion of social housing tenants in England receiving Housing Benefit declined from nine out of ten among those with a gross weekly income of under £100, to eight out of ten among those with a weekly income of £100 to £199, to approximately half among those with an income of £200 to £299, and to one-fifth among those with a weekly income of £300 or more. Thus, Housing Benefit is highly targeted on the poor (Stephens 2005).

Figure 4: Percentage of tenants in receipt of Housing Benefit, by gross weekly income

Gross weekly income*	Council tenants	Housing association tenants
Under £100	92	89
£100 to £199	82	83
£200 to £299	52	55
£300 or more	22	21

* Gross weekly income of 'household reference person' (and partner)

Source: Survey of English Housing 2005/06.

Low take-up is well known as one of the potential disadvantages of means-tested benefits (Deacon and Bradshaw 1983). However, the take-up rate of Housing Benefit is relatively high. Estimates made by statisticians in the DWP consistently indicate that approximately nine out of ten entitled social housing tenants in Great Britain are in receipt of Housing Benefit. For example, the latest figures suggest that the caseload take-up rate in 2006/07 was between 87 per cent and 92 per cent (DWP 2008). Although Housing Benefit take-up data for other countries is limited, the data that is available indicates that the take-up rate is much higher in Britain than elsewhere (Kemp 1997).

The impact of Housing Benefit

Housing Benefit helps to improve the affordability of social housing for low-income tenants. This is illustrated in Figure 5, below, which shows rent as a percentage of gross income, both before and after Housing Benefit, averaged across *all* households (including non-recipients). It indicates that, calculated across social housing tenants as a whole, Housing Benefit roughly halves rent-to-income ratios (Stephens 2005).

Figure 5: Rents as a percentage of income before and after Housing Benefit*

	Council tenants	Housing association tenants
Before Housing Benefit	26.2	30.9
After Housing Benefit	12.8	15.7
Reduction	-51%	-49%

* Averaged across all tenants in each tenure.

Source: Stephens (2005) based on Survey of English Housing data for 2001/02.

The data in Figure 5, above, under-estimates the impact of Housing Benefit because they are averaged across each sub-sector as a whole, not just people who are recipients. In practice, the amount by which Housing Benefit reduces rent-to-income ratios in social housing varies according to a range of factors, especially income and whether or not the recipient has non-dependants living in their household. Tenants who are living on means-tested income support benefits and have no non-dependent children living with them, will normally be entitled to have their full rent met by Housing Benefit. For these very low-income tenants, the rent-to-income ratio will therefore be nil.

Figure 6, below, shows median rents after Housing Benefit, according to four levels of gross weekly income. It can be seen that the net rent after Housing Benefit is nil or almost nil for tenants whose income is under £200 per week, and thereafter rises as income increases. This pattern reflects the means-tested (income-related) nature of the scheme. Almost by definition it gives more help to tenants on the lowest incomes and less to those who are relatively better-off (Gibbs and Kemp 1993; Jones 2006).

Figure 6: Median rents* after Housing Benefit by gross weekly income

Gross weekly income~	Council tenants £pw	Housing association tenants £pw
Under £100	0	0
£100 to £199	2	0
£200 to £299	41	44
£300 or more	54	65
All	19	27

* Median rents are based on all households in each income band, not just those on Housing Benefit.
~ Gross weekly income of household reference person (and partner)
Source: Survey of English Housing 2005/06.

Since the availability of Housing Benefit makes rents more affordable to social housing tenants, it should also help to minimise the incidence of rent arrears. This is confirmed by research reported in Ford and Seavers (1998) which found that, controlling for other variables, receipt of Housing Benefit reduced the odds of housing association tenants being in rent arrears. However, the administration of Housing Benefit is fraught with difficulties, including delays in the processing of both new claims and changes in circumstances in existing claims. The scheme also has a relatively high error rate, among other problems. These delays and errors can result in financial hardship for claimants, with the result that some end up falling behind with their rent (Audit Commission 2002). Indeed, the *Survey of English Housing 2004/05* found that one-quarter of social housing tenants who were behind with the rent (either at the time of the survey or in the previous 12 months) cited problems with Housing Benefit as a reason for their arrears.

Housing Benefit as an in-work benefit

In his report, John Hills (2007) highlighted the very high level of worklessness among tenants living in social housing. This issue is examined in detail by Robinson in Chapter 7. The aim here is to consider the potential impact of Housing Benefit on incentives to take up paid employment or to increase hours of work.

An important feature of Housing Benefit is that, as well as retired and workless households, people who are in low-paid employment or self-employment are also eligible to apply for it. Because Housing Benefit is an in-work, as well as an out-of-work, benefit, it can help to make work pay and thereby prevent the 'unemployment trap' from occurring. Often conflated with the poverty trap, the unemployment trap refers to situations where moving from welfare to work would result in a household being worse-off (or little better-off) financially. In general, Housing Benefit helps to ensure that households are better-off in paid work than living on out-of-work benefits. However, when in-work expenses (eg, for travel to work, the purchase of work clothes and especially child care) are taken into account, the financial gains from working may disappear (Stephens 2005).

High rents are often thought to create an unemployment trap (Social Security Committee 2000), but in social housing this is less of a problem than in the private rental sector, as rents are generally below market levels. Moreover, since for social housing tenants Housing Benefit increases pound for pound as rents increase, the move from welfare to low-paid work should leave households no worse-off. Nevertheless, very high rents do raise the amount of earnings that are required to lift people out of entitlement to Housing Benefit (Cannizzaro 2007).

Despite being an in-work benefit, Housing Benefit is not especially successful in providing help with housing costs for tenants in paid work. The take-up rate for Housing Benefit among people in employment is muchlower than for other eligible claimants. Thus, estimates made by the DWP (2008) suggest that the take-up rate among people in employment is only in the range of 41–54 per cent. This compares with a rate of 92–96 per cent among people who are not in employment.[6] Qualitative research suggests that some people assume they would not be entitled to Housing Benefit when in work (Ford et al 1996). In addition, some entitled claimants in work appear to be put off by the delays and other problems with the administration of the scheme.

Problems with the administration of Housing Benefit are a potential barrier to taking up paid work, especially for people who are caught up in the 'low pay, no pay' cycle (moving back and forth between temporary jobs and welfare). For people in this situation, the critical issue is not simply how much better-off they would be if they took up a job, but also the impact of moving into work, and of returning to welfare when the job comes to an end, on their Housing Benefit claim. The fact that Housing Benefit can take several weeks to be recalculated following a change of circumstances, such as taking up a job or losing one, adds to the uncertainty, financial risk and hassles associated with moving into work and returning to welfare when it comes to an end. The DWP has introduced a host of reforms that aim to simplify administration and make things easier for recipients who take up a

---

[6] The take-up figures by employment are for social and private tenants together.

job. Nevertheless, despite these improvements, Housing Benefit does not yet provide a secure pillar for tenants on the margins of the labour market.

Moreover, for people who are working Housing Benefit contributes to the 'poverty trap'. This is the situation where households in low-paid work and claiming Housing Benefit would be little better-off from increasing their earnings by working longer hours or receiving a modest pay rise. As a means-tested social security benefit, entitlement to Housing Benefit decreases as income rises (and vice versa). Recipients lose 65 pence of their Housing Benefit for an extra £1 of take-home pay. This is a very high rate of benefit withdrawal compared with the Housing Benefit schemes in other advanced economies (Kemp 1997).

Recipients in low-paid work not only lose some of their Housing Benefit when they earn more; they also lose some of their other income-related benefits and tax credits as well. In addition, they typically pay Income Tax and National Insurance on their extra earnings. As a result of these deductions, Housing Benefit recipients may be little better-off financially, despite an increase in gross earnings. In some cases, the 'marginal deduction rate' can exceed 90 per cent, but rates of 70 per cent are more common (Wilcox 1993).

One way of reducing the high marginal deduction rate for working people in receipt of Housing Benefit would be to cut the income taper. However, doing so would extend Housing Benefit further up the income scale and thereby increase the number of people affected by the poverty trap. As a way of reducing the poverty trap, decreasing the taper would also be poorly targeted since it would benefit all claimants with some income over income support levels, and not just those who are working. It would also be very expensive. The money might be better spent on simplifying the scheme in ways that reduce the financial risks associated with taking up low-paid and temporary jobs. The introduction of fixed periods of awards, or disregarding increases in incomes along the lines of the Working Tax Credit, are two possible routes towards that goal, although both would have cost implications.

A Local Housing Allowance?

Following a trial in 18 local authorities, a new Local Housing Allowance was introduced nationally in April 2008, in place of Housing Benefit for private tenants. Social housing tenants remain in the old Housing Benefit scheme. The essential characteristic of the Local Housing Allowance is that the maximum Housing Benefit entitlement is no longer based on the claimant's rent. Instead, within each local market area (as defined by The Rent Service), there is a standard maximum amount for all claimants which varies only by household size and composition.

Claimants whose income is at, or below, the 'applicable amounts' – in essence, the rates for the means-tested income support benefits – receive the full standard allowance.[7] For people whose income is above their applicable amount, the Local Housing Allowance tapers out at the same rate – 65 per cent of net income – as in the Housing Benefit scheme. The Local Housing Allowance is normally paid to the claimant, but can be paid directly to the landlord where the tenant is deemed to be vulnerable, or is eight or more weeks in arrears with their rent.

The rationale for this reform is to build choice and responsibility into Housing Benefit (DWP 2002). The Government hopes that the Local Housing Allowance will encourage recipients to make trade-offs between quality and price when looking for accommodation in the rental housing market. The Local Housing Allowance is both simpler and more transparent than Housing Benefit for private tenants, not least because it avoids the need for complex determinations by The Rent Service about the reasonableness of the claimant's rent and the size of their accommodation. The Government also hopes that knowing in advance how much Local Housing Allowance they will get, and having it paid to them instead of their landlord, will empower recipients and encourage them to take more responsibility for their budgeting and rent payment obligations.

Thus, there are now two Housing Benefit schemes, one for private tenants and another for people living in social housing. The experience of implementing the Local Housing Allowance in the pathfinder areas was largely successful and this raises the question of whether a Local Housing Allowance could or should be introduced for social housing tenants. Although the Government initially anticipated moving towards the introduction of a Local Housing Allowance for social housing, it subsequently put this aspiration on hold (DWP 2006). That decision is perhaps not surprising as the evidence suggests that extending the Local Housing Allowance to social rented housing may not be easy. This is because rents are determined, and tenancies are allocated, very differently in social housing from in the private sector, and in ways that are less suitable for paying a standard allowance irrespective of claimants' actual rent (Kemp 2006).

A fundamental premise underlying the design of the Local Housing Allowance is that claimants are able to make choices, or trade-offs, between quality of accommodation and the price they have to pay for it. For this to happen, there needs to be a more consistent relationship than often exists in social housing at present between the attributes of a property (in terms of its size, amenities, location, etc) and the rent charged for it. Moreover, there are differences between the rents charged by local authorities and those charged by housing associations letting homes within the same area. The result is that different rents may be charged for broadly similar properties (Wilcox 1997).

---

[7] Provided they do not have non-dependants living with them.

These inconsistencies mean that it may not be easy to make the sorts of trade-offs in social housing that are implied in setting a standard Local Housing Allowance. It will also make it difficult to set a single Local Housing Allowance level for all social housing tenants in each local authority area. In England, these problems have been recognised by the Government and a long-term process of rent restructuring and harmonisation in social housing is underway. But this process is expected to take many years and, in practice, may prove to be difficult to fully achieve (Walker and Marsh 2002).

The Local Housing Allowance is also premised on the assumption that claimants will be able to move accommodation in order to exercise choice and make trade-offs between rent and quality. In other words, the assumption is that, once the Local Housing Allowance has been set, claimants could choose to move to somewhere more expensive and make up the difference out of their own pocket. Likewise, they could choose to move somewhere cheaper and thereby make a saving. But, despite moves toward choice-based lettings (discussed by Pawson in Chapter 6), claimants have much less scope to make such trade-offs, or move accommodation, in social housing than in the private rental sector. Consequently, many existing social housing tenants are not in a position to shop around for accommodation (Kemp 2000).

In summary, it will be difficult to introduce a Local Housing Allowance that relies on the operation of a market when an administered system, rather than a market, is in place. Making social housing more market-like in order to facilitate the introduction of a Local Housing Allowance would raise fundamental questions about the nature of this tenure, including the extent to which it is primarily focused on helping those people who are in most need (Kemp 2006).

Paying Housing Benefit

Although the Government currently has no plans to extend the Local Housing Allowance to social housing, it does want to encourage the payment of Housing Benefit directly to claimants living in council and housing association accommodation (DWP 2006). The present situation is that all claimants renting their home from a local authority, and approximately nine out of ten renting from a housing association, do not get paid their Housing Benefit – instead it is sent directly to their landlord.[8]

The Welfare Reform Act 2007 allows regulations to be made that could be used to require that Housing Benefit payments be made to claimants. The Government hopes that paying Housing Benefit to claimants would promote personal responsibility and empower people to budget for themselves. They think it would also help workless tenants to develop the skills they will need when they move into paid work. And they believe it would encourage

[8] In the case of council tenants, the benefits department pays the money directly to their rent account.

claimants to open bank accounts and pay their rent by standing order or direct debit, thereby helping to promote financial inclusion and payment modernisation (DWP 2006).

In contrast, organisations representing landlords, mortgage lenders and other critics fear that claimants will spend their Housing Benefit on other things rather than use it to pay their rent. As a result, rent arrears, and hence evictions and homelessness, would, or could, increase. An increase in rent arrears could, in turn, have serious consequences for landlords' cash flows and undermine the ability of housing associations to repay their loans (Ricketts 2006). This argument implicitly assumes that Housing Benefit claimants cannot be relied upon to pay the rent if the benefit is given to them rather than to their landlord (Irvine et al 2007).

The experience of the Local Housing Allowance pathfinders for private tenants suggests that most Housing Benefit claimants can be trusted to pay the rent if the benefit is paid to them and not to their landlord. The proportion of recipients that were personally receiving their benefit (instead of it being paid directly to the landlord) increased, from approximately one-half prior to the Local Housing Allowance to about nine out of ten after its introduction (Roberts et al 2006). This substantial increase in payment to the claimant did not result in a significant rise in rent arrears (Walker 2005). Meanwhile, although there were some initial teething problems (Citizens Advice 2005), the nine local authorities where the Local Housing Allowance was being evaluated were able to identify 'vulnerable' recipients who could not manage their finances, for whom direct payment to the landlord remained appropriate. Moreover, there was no evidence to suggest that homelessness had increased among Local Housing Allowance recipients in the pathfinder areas (Walker 2006).

However, the proportion of tenants who might be deemed to be vulnerable is likely to be higher in social housing than in the private rental sector. That suggests the proportion of people for whom payment to the claimants is appropriate is likely to be smaller in social housing than was the case in the Local Housing Allowance pathfinders. But it seems unlikely that the majority of social housing tenants are incapable of budgeting responsibly, despite living on low or modest incomes.

Qualitative research with 82 social and private tenants on Housing Benefit suggests that some tenants would have difficulty in adjusting to having their Housing Benefit paid to them, either because of the extra hassle it would involve or because they were worried about spending the money on something else instead of the rent. If Housing Benefit is routinely paid to non-vulnerable social housing tenants, claimants who have difficulty in adjusting will need intensive support, including money management advice. Procedures will need to be developed that make it possible to quickly identify the minority of claimants who are so vulnerable that their benefit needs to continue being paid to their landlord (Irvine et al 2007).

Conclusion

Housing Benefit plays a very important role in social housing. It enables low-income tenants to afford their rent and underpins the financial viability of social housing landlords. The scheme also helps to make work pay, albeit at the cost of contributing to high marginal deduction rates for workers whose pay increases. The beneficial impact of Housing Benefit is reduced somewhat by the problems associated with the administration of the scheme, the extent of which varies quite widely between local authorities. For this reason, and because of low take-up among tenants in low-paid employment, Housing Benefit is not working very well for people on the margins of the labour market. Further reform, including benefit simplification, is required in order for Housing Benefit to provide a secure pillar for people moving from welfare to work, especially for those caught up in the 'low pay, no pay' cycle.

The introduction of a flat-rate Local Housing Allowance in social housing, mirroring that which has been introduced for private tenants, is scarcely feasible in a tenure that gives priority to the households most in need and charges below market rents. While there may be scope for paying Housing Benefit to social housing tenants instead of their landlords, this option is unlikely to be viable for the minority of claimants who are vulnerable and unable to manage their finances without getting into debt.

Peter Kemp is the Barnett Professor of Social Policy and a Professorial Fellow of St Cross College, Oxford.

References

Audit Commission, 2002. *Learning from inspection: Housing Benefit administration.* London: Audit Commission.

Cannizzaro, A., 2007. *Impacts of rents on Housing Benefit and work incentives.* DWP Working Paper No. 38. Leeds: Corporate Document Services.

Citizens Advice, 2005. *Early days: CAB evidence on the Local Housing Allowance.* London: Citizens Advice.

Deacon, A. and Bradshaw, J., 1983. *Reserved for the poor: the means test in British social policy.* Oxford: Basil Blackwell and Martin Robertson.

DWP, 2002. *Building choice and responsibility: a radical agenda for housing benefit.* London: DWP.

DWP, 2005. *Work and pensions statistics 2004.* London: DWP.

DWP, 2006. *A new deal for welfare: empowering people to work.* London: DWP.

DWP, 2008. *Income related benefits. Estimates of take-up in 2006–07.* London: DWP.

Ford, J., Kempson, E. and England, J., 1996. *Into work? The impact of housing costs and the benefit system on people's decision to work.* York: JRF.

Ford, J. and Seavers, J., 1998. *Housing associations and rent arrears.* Coventry: CIH.

Gibbs, I. and Kemp, P.A., 1993. Housing Benefit and income redistribution. *Urban Studies,* 30(1), p.63–72.

Hills, J., 2007. *Ends and means: the future roles of social housing in England.* CASE Report 34. London: CASE and LSE. Available at: http://tinyurl.com/24ms5b

Irvine, A., Kemp, P.A. and Nice, K., 2007. *The payment of Housing Benefit: what do claimants think?* Coventry: CIH and JRF.

Jones, F., 2006. The effects of taxes and benefits on household income, 2004/05. *Economic Trends,* 630, May, p.53–98.

Kemp, P.A., 1997. *A comparative study of housing allowances.* London: TSO.

Kemp, P.A., 2000. *Shopping incentives and Housing Benefit reform.* Coventry: CIH and JRF.

Kemp, P.A., 2006. Housing Benefit: Great Britain in comparative perspective. *Public Finance and Management,* 6(1), p.65–87.

Kemp, P.A., 2007. Housing Benefit in Britain: a troubled history and uncertain future. In P.A. Kemp, ed. *Housing allowances in comparative perspective.* Bristol: The Policy Press.

Ricketts, A., 2006. Eviction fears over direct payments. Inside Housing, 3 Mar.

Roberts, S. et al,. 2006. *Living with the LHA: claimants' experiences after 15 months in the nine pathfinder areas.* Local Housing Allowance Evaluation Report No. 9. Leeds: Corporate Document Services.

Social Security Committee, 2000. *Housing Benefit,* Session 1999–2000, Sixth report. London: TSO.

Stephens, M., 2005. An assessment of the British Housing Benefit system. *European Journal of Housing Policy,* 5(2), p.111–129.

Walker, B., 2005. *15 months on: an interim evaluation of running the LHA in the nine pathfinder areas.* Local Housing Allowance Evaluation Report No. 8. Leeds: Corporate Document Services.

Walker, B., 2006. *Local Housing Allowance final evaluation: implementation and delivery in the nine pathfinder areas.* Local Housing Allowance Evaluation Report No. 10. Leeds: Corporate Document Services.

Walker, B. and Marsh, A., 2002. Setting the rents of social housing: the impact and implications of rent restructuring in England. *Urban Studies,* 40(10), p.2023–2047.

Wilcox, S., 1993. *Housing Benefit and the disincentive to work.* York: JRF.

Wilcox, S., 1997. Incoherent rents. In S. Wilcox, ed. *Housing finance review 1997/98.* York: JRF.

Wilcox, S. ed., 2005. *UK housing review 2005/06.* Coventry: CIH and CML.

Chapter 5

Social housing and spatial segregation

Keith Kintrea

Introduction

Part of John Hills' remit was to examine what social housing could do to create genuinely mixed communities (Hills 2007, p.13). This is in line with the emphasis in government policy on housing, regeneration and planning. Following that policy, and consistent with the propositions of most of the research in this area (Blasius et al 2007), Hills focused on income (rather than age, gender or ethnicity, for example) as the key ingredient of 'mix'. He identified that a theoretical benefit of social housing was its potential to break the link between household income and location, therefore allowing people with low incomes to live in areas that they could not afford if housing was distributed by the market alone. However, his evidence showed the opposite. In practice, social housing concentrated poverty, rather than dispersed it. In particular, concentration was associated with the continuing dominance of spatially distinctive, council-built estates from the era of mass housing construction, and the strong role of social housing in meeting housing need.

This chapter will examine the evidence about whether, and if so how, social housing contributes towards the segregation of low-income households, and will consider to what extent this might be disadvantageous. It also looks at what can be done about segregation, examining Hills' proposals and others.

Segregation and the concentration of poverty

Segregation concerns the spatial separation of people according to their social and/or economic position. The essence of the problem of segregation is the interplay of housing systems and labour market-derived inequalities and, for policy makers interested in alleviating segregation, these are both relevant areas for intervention. However, because the origin of economic inequalities lies most fundamentally in the labour market, housing processes can only play a secondary role in alleviating inequality. Also, although low-income households are geographically concentrated, the majority of poor people do not live in poor areas as Palmer et al (2006) show.

Nevertheless, there are trends towards more socio-spatial segregation in the UK, as elsewhere. Greater inequalities in labour markets, a significant group who are distanced from the labour market, the separation of the poorest (the marginalised or the socially excluded) from mainstream society, and poor levels of socialisation and sometimes outbreaks of disorder among this group, are all trends identified internationally (eg Fainstein et al 1992; Mingione 1996; Sassen 2001) (see Atkinson et al 2005). All of these tendencies come to the surface in the shape of areas of concentrated disadvantage.

In the background is the question of overall poverty rates and levels of inequality which, as noted in Chapter 1, are higher than in many other European countries. Although there have been improvements for some households and individuals, in the last 15 years poverty rates in the UK appear to have risen rather than fallen although there are fewer people who are very poor (Dorling et al 2007). But the same analysis also suggests that the wealthy have become wealthier, so that society is continuing to become more unequal.

There are also strong and well-established regional differences. For example, Dorling et al (2007), working on the basis of bespoke 'tracts' of 45,000 people on average, report that areas where more than 40 per cent of the population are 'breadline poor' are only found in inner London, cities in the north and midlands of England, central Scotland, and in the valleys of South Wales. Working at the smaller scale of electoral wards (an average of 5,000 people, but usually much bigger in cities), Lupton (2005, Table 2) found that 64 per cent of all wards in England where more than 40 per cent of the population were 'work poor' (ie people of working age who were not working or studying) were in the North East and North West, which contained only 17 per cent of all wards nationally.

Local studies between 1971 and 2001, reviewed by Dorling et al (2007), suggest that patterns of segregation between the poorer and better-off households had become more exaggerated over time in the UK's city regions. For example, in city regions in the north and midlands of England, and in the Glasgow area, poverty levels for sub-areas rose within the city boundary, while in the wealthier areas in the surrounding suburbs they remained stable. In London and the surrounding Home Counties they comment on 'an increasingly intense bulls-eye effect' with deepening concentrations of poverty in inner and east London, and rising concentrations of wealth in the outer areas. Altogether, across most conurbations, the conclusion they draw is that segregation of low-income from better-off households has been increasing.

There are no official measures of segregation. However, with respect to multiple deprivation, the local concentration measure identifies hot spots of deprivation, ie areas amounting to ten per cent of the local population which exhibit particularly deep deprivation. A ranking of the 50 most deprived local authorities in England on this measure shows that 28 are in the North West or the North East, and a further 16 are in Yorkshire and Humberside or in the East or West Midlands. That leaves just six in the rest of the country, including two London boroughs (Noble et al 2008, Table 5.4).

An examination of segregation in England using indices of dissimilarity based on wards (Meen et al 2005) concluded that the greatest segregation within local authority areas is found in older industrial locations in the north of England, such as Middlesbrough, Stockton, Preston and West Lancashire. This is consistent with the deprivation hot spot locations, and also with regions identified by Lupton (2005) as having the greatest proportion of poor wards.

At a local level, it is the housing system that translates economic inequalities into spatial segregation, and concentrates the distribution of low-income households. Owner occupation has grown to about 70 per cent of households in the UK, while social housing has fallen to under 20 per cent, and households within it are increasingly poor. Over the post-war period, social housing has shifted – or been shifted by policy – from providing for the ordinary family to becoming a residualised welfare safety net, mainly housing those with few other choices. Using an index based on education and occupation, Feinstein et al (2008, Figures 7 and 8) show that, up to 1965, the proportion of the population in social housing rose across all social backgrounds, although it was less marked among the more advantaged. After that, up to 2003, the proportion of all groups in social housing fell, except for the least advantaged quintile, for which it rose. The same study also shows a fall in the proportion of the least advantaged quintile in owner occupation since 1975 (Feinstein et al 2008, Figures 9 and 10). At a European level, although there are no formal income tests for entering social housing in the UK, Stephens et al (2003) show that, relative to its size, British social housing contains a greater proportion of poor households than other Western European countries (see also Stephens, Chapter 2).

That social housing increasingly concentrates low-income households is the result of three tendencies. Firstly, strongly as a result of policy, allocation of housing since the 1970s has been based on needs, and social housing has become an important destination for officially-recognised homeless households (see Fitzpatrick, Chapter 3). Secondly, the areas with the most social housing outside London are industrial cities and towns which were the most badly hit by industrial restructuring from the 1970s onwards. Therefore, older tenants have become poorer in situ (Lupton 2003), and younger people struggle to come to terms with a changed labour market. The upshot of this, as Hills (2007, Figure 9.1) reports, is that in 2004/05 almost 70 per cent of households in social housing were in the bottom 40 per cent of the income range. Thirdly, the built form of social housing still appears largely in the form of estates. This is mainly as a result of historic patterns of development combined with the tendency for sales to sitting tenants under the right to buy to be disproportionately high in areas where there was already less social housing. Palmer et al (2006, Tables 42a and 42b) report that social housing tenants in Britain have, on average, half of their neighbours who are also social housing tenants, compared to only 12 per cent for those who are not social housing tenants. Although in recent years there has been comparatively little new social housebuilding (see Bramley, Chapter 8), what there is continues to contribute to segregation. Bramley et al (2007, p.18) point out that, 'there has been a fairly striking concentration of new social housing output in the most deprived neighbourhoods'.

The areas where social housing is most clustered tend to be deprived in other respects (Hills 2007, Table 9.3). In fact, the proportion of social housing in the most deprived areas of England grew, and the proportion in the least deprived areas declined, between 1991 and 2004. Kearns and Mason (2007) also show that social housing is associated with a wide range of neighbourhood disadvantages.

The impacts of concentrated disadvantage

A key question underlying this discussion is whether the concentration of poverty matters. Since William Julius Wilson (1987), using evidence from Chicago, proposed that to be poor in a poor neighbourhood compounded people's poverty, neighbourhood effects has become a strong theme of research. The core of the idea is that the locality is an important arena in which beliefs, attitudes and expectations are constructed through local social relationships, and these can have impacts on people's life chances. While neighbourhood effects can emerge, in principle, in any kind of area, the key concern of research and policy is the potential negative impacts that arise in poor areas.

The idea rests on three propositions (Atkinson and Kintrea 2004). The first is that people with low incomes live in relative isolation in their own areas. The second is that a bonding type of social capital dominates in poor areas, which is constraining and inward-looking although it helps people to 'get by', compared to a bridging type of social capital that is found in greater quantities elsewhere, which helps people to 'get on' (Portes 2000). The third proposition is that the norms which develop in conditions of isolation in poor areas are a barrier to social inclusion; there is a levelling down of aspirations and expectations.

Analysts of welfare systems have tended to place the UK among a group of Anglo-Saxon countries where inequalities are relatively wide and the housing system more segregated (Kemeny 1995). Arguably then, compared to other European countries, the UK has more potential for neighbourhood effects because it has a more distinctive set of poorer neighbourhoods and a more residualised social housing system that constrains a greater proportion of low-income households to live among others like themselves.

Findings on these questions from quantitative and qualitative studies in matched pairs of neighbourhoods – deprived and more socially mixed – in

Glasgow and Edinburgh can be summarised from Atkinson and Kintrea (2001, 2004) and Atkinson et al (2005). It was clear that the deprived areas were relatively socially isolated from the rest of their cities in several respects, so the condition existed for a localised social dynamic to develop. These areas were isolated in the opinion of outsiders, who stigmatised the relevant neighbourhoods and avoided going there. Although there was a high turnover of residents, and an exodus of the more ambitious and economically successful, a core of stable, poor households remained who were largely untouched by the throughput. One interviewee described these processes as 'skimming off the best and leaving the dross in a white working class ghetto'.

Many of the residents did not travel very much to other areas of the city, partly because they lacked resources, and partly because they lacked reasons, skills and confidence. Various residents told us that the rest of the city, or specifically the city centre, was 'out of bounds' or 'on another planet'. Of the relatively few who participated in the labour market, a very high proportion worked locally, mainly in service jobs.

The social networks that existed in the poor estates were limited in their reach. They were cohesive places in that many people had local friends and acquaintances, but they were also fractured by crime and antisocial behaviour. This heightened a sense of mutual support and survival, but many people lacked strong networks beyond the estates. This is consistent with MacDonald and Marsh's (2005) research in disadvantaged estates in the north-east of England. There was bonding social capital, but not much evidence of being able to use bridging social capital to 'get on'. Even within the estates, many people were disconnected from each other across short distances, compounded by territorial behaviour (see Kintrea et al 2008). Many residents were not socially or economically mobile, and often had no expectation that upward mobility was possible, especially in a context of widespread economic change that had removed the industrial base and sponsored widespread unemployment.

These Scottish findings that suggest that neighbourhood effects are real are echoed in recent studies of deprived neighbourhoods in England (for example, North and Syrett 2006; MacDonald and Marsh 2005; Macdonald et al 2004; see also Robinson, Chapter 7). However, research in London has indicated that the disadvantages associated with residence in poor areas there are much fewer, and the problem of communities being inward-looking and disconnected are not so evident (Atkinson et al 2005). This can probably be explained by differences in the spatial structure of London, and the weaker concentration (but not extensity) of deprivation, and the impacts of a pressured market on the locational decisions of better-off households who are forced to live in closer proximity to disadvantaged estates.

It is hard to get adequate statistical data to measure independent neighbourhood effects, in particular to separate out their influence from that of household and individual characteristics (Feinstein et al 2008). In the UK, Buck (2001), McCulloch (2001) and Bolster et al (2007) have all used the British Household Panel Survey, albeit in different ways, to make comparisons over the life-cycle between people that have lived in deprived areas and those that have not. Buck (2001) found that people's chance of starting a job, or leaving poverty, were decreased by living in a poor area, while their chances of re-entering poverty were higher. Bolster et al (2007), looking at income, found no evidence that neighbourhood disadvantage affected income growth over time.

Clearly, the issue is not wholly settled but the international evidence tends to the view that there are grounds for accepting that neighbourhood effects exist and are detrimental to social equity (Galster 2007). A collection of papers using varied data sets, and statistical techniques and controls, from several European countries also all support the existence of neighbourhood effects (Blasius et al 2007). What this indicates is that there are good grounds for seeking to desegregate poverty.

Ways forward

So, can the segregation of the poorest neighbourhoods that seem to bring additional disadvantages to poorer people be countered by policy? Conventionally, the approach to deprived social renting estates has been to carry out regeneration programmes, typically a combination of physical improvements and a range of social and economic projects. A recent review (Kintrea 2007) suggests that this inward-looking approach has had limited success, partly because of the distance that has to be crossed to bring the worst estates up to even average levels of prosperity. Also, the longstanding process of residualisation of social housing has continued in the face of regeneration and, as discussed above, segregation between income groups has grown.

Hills (2007) compiled several suggestions about how to turn council-built estates into mixed neighbourhoods. He recognises that it is important to consider how income profiles might be changed in the social rented sector, by extending tenants' participation in the labour market, consistent with the analysis that the root of inequalities lies in the labour market. His own report shows that only 32 per cent of tenants have a job, with only two-thirds of those tenants working full-time (Hills 2007, Figure 5.4). He proposes a more integrated approach to the provision of social housing and housing benefits, and more support for joining the labour market, with a view to removing some of the discouragements to coming off benefit. Although this could make an important difference, it does not fully recognise the large numbers in social housing who are not able to work, or are above retirement age. His own report shows that retirees are the largest single employment status group among social renters, while the second largest is economically inactive people of working age, two-thirds of whom are lone parents. He also shows that over 40 per cent of households have someone who has a serious medical condition or is disabled, double the proportion of any other tenure. The other problems which do not surface are the wide variation in labour markets across England, and the significant differences in scale of social housing.

Hills' other suggestions are less original. He considers various ways to reinvent social housing and, in doing so, make it more attractive to higher-income groups, by creating greater equality between the benefits offered by private and social housing respectively. This was proposed by the Institute for Public Policy Research (IPPR) (2000), which suggested that housing associations and local authorities should offer market rent options, whereas Hills also suggests more use of equity-sharing tenures. The problem with this proposal is that there has been no let-up of the key role of social housing in meeting needs, notwithstanding a recent fall in the number of statutorily homeless households (see Fitzpatrick, Chapter 3). Without spending more on increasing the supply of social housing far beyond existing commitments (see Bramley, Chapter 8), it is difficult to see how an extension to more affluent groups could be justified. It is also difficult to see how those with choices are going to be attracted to rent in low-status areas among low-income people if there are other alternatives (see Monk et al, Chapter 9).

A further possible approach is to diversify housing estates through selective demolition and replacement with more upmarket housing. A key question is how much diversification is necessary to transform the social dynamics of housing estates. In practice, the reconstruction of social housing areas has frequently been piecemeal and incremental, and often not well planned, relying on opportunistic insertion of low-cost private housing (Atkinson and Kintrea 2002). Kearns and Mason (2007) consider the association between social housing and neighbourhood problems, and suggest the reduction of social housing to perhaps one-eighth of the stock in any one neighbourhood. Essentially, this would require the dispersal of social housing, rather than its dilution in existing estates.

Management-led approaches are also sometimes promoted as a way forward. This means close attention to the basics, such as dwelling quality and repair services; an emphasis on tenancy management to combat antisocial behaviour; better neighbourhood management, including a focus on crime; as well as taking care of the physical environment outside the home. Changes to allocations, including choice-based lettings, are also suggested as ways to both diversify residents and protect against concentrations of difficult households. Hills (2007) believes that these kinds of changes are important. However, given the very longstanding difficulty of making inroads through regeneration into improving the relative position of social housing estates, it is hard to believe that these kinds of changes will make much difference to social profiles. Even Tunstall and Coulter (2006), who are positive about 'turning the tide' in council-built estates through sustained investment and improved management, are sceptical about the effectiveness of this approach in low-demand regions that are, as discussed above, the most badly affected by socio-spatial segregation and probably also by neighbourhood effects.

As well as looking at how existing concentrations of poverty might be broken up, as Hills does, it is also important to consider how future concentrations might be avoided. Atkinson and Kintrea (2002) suggested other ways for policy to take desegregation more seriously through changes to housing and planning policy. In England, current official policy relating to planning for housing places an obligation on spatial strategies at regional, local authority and site level to plan for a mix of housing (DCLG 2006, p.9). This has been accompanied by the Mixed Communities Initiative, a set of pilot projects currently under evaluation.

There are three main contexts within which mixed communities might be created, and for each of these it is fair to say that policy is not yet mature. Firstly, there are master-planned new communities. Even if the current scale of social housing development is modest in a historical context, developments such as the Thames Gateway and the controversial eco-towns present opportunities for good planning. For these, there is now a body of good practice advice and examples from experience to draw upon, best expressed in Bailey et al (2006). Master-planned new communities usually start with a site that is more or less open because former uses have been cleared. They are then able to overcome the path dependency that has often locked places with greater continuity into a particular social status. Mixed communities have been created successfully because of clear objectives at the point of initiation and, typically, private developers and housing associations have been brought together on that basis.

Master-planned mixed communities usually have a lead organisation that shapes the scheme and promotes adherence to the vision and, in the larger and more ambitious schemes, other local amenities, such as shopping, community centres, and primary schools, are also part of the plan. In the longer term, it is recognised that such communities also need overt management (unlike most residential areas), particularly to consider approaches to letting social housing, tackling crime and antisocial behaviour, and maintaining and managing the physical environment. The evidence is clear that such schemes can work (Bailey et al 2006).

There are perhaps two main misgivings. The first is that it remains a significant challenge, particularly in inner city areas, to attract more affluent families (Silverman et al 2005). Private developers typically build small units which are not suitable for children. In contrast, the social housing in mixed-tenure developments often has relatively high numbers of children. This is because, with a general shortage of family homes for rent, housing associations take advantage of new building opportunities to provide larger homes which are then fully occupied, consistent with the bedroom standard (see Monk et al, Chapter 9). This implies that socialisation among children and young people in local schools, or in the neighbourhood, may still predominantly take place between those who come from relatively poor, social renting backgrounds, as the more affluent still head for the suburbs when they have children. This is important because there is a growing understanding that the impact of neighbourhood effects is greatest during childhood and adolescence (Galster et al 2007). The second misgiving is that, in pursuit of social sustainability and to head-off neighbour disputes between owners and social housing tenants, there is a temptation by managers to avoid placing the most disadvantaged households in mixed-tenure areas (Bailey et al 2006).

The second kind of environment in which mixed communities might be created is new development areas that are led by the private sector. In these circumstances, the ability of public policy to shape housing mix, and social mix outcomes, is much more limited. Since the 1990s, there has been the possibility of influencing the extent to which new developments provide affordable housing by specifying requirements for affordable housing in area-wide development plans, and then using these as a basis to formulate planning agreements with developers using section 106 of the Town and Country Planning Act 1990 (Crook et al 2002). As developers would almost always prefer to build for market sale without hindrance, to a large extent the policy has rested upon the extent to which it can be made robust enough to withstand appeal processes. After ten years of operation, the more successful planning authorities have achieved a high proportion of all affordable housing benefiting from this process. But it is difficult to make such policies work in lower demand markets of the North, where, as we have discussed above, the greatest segregation occurs. The current (2008) slump in housing starts will also impact dramatically on the success of this policy.

A recent policy development is to include mixed communities as a legitimate object of planning processes (DCLG 2006) but it seems doubtful whether this will add all that much to existing provision. For a start, the emphasis is very much on house sizes and types, and not income groups, except that some income differences might be expected to be represented across house types. It is possible for planning authorities, for the first time, to include tenure as a planning concern, which is a significant departure from previously 'tenure blind' policies. However, social housing requires to be funded, as well as strategised.

Finally, it is worth mentioning some other possible approaches to promoting greater socio-spatial integration. Portable capital subsidies would enable social housing tenants to choose houses in the private sector, which their landlord would then buy and rent back to them (Atkinson and Kintrea 2002). More widely, as Hills mentions, social landlords, instead of procuring additions to their stocks through contracts for building new estates, could proceed by buying housing on the open market, therefore diversifying the range of areas in which houses were available for rent. In the current (2008) depression in the housing market, £200 million has been made available to housing associations in England to buy up unsold private developers' houses (DCLG 2008), although this is motivated more by reducing costs and supporting the market rather than promoting social mix. There is some concern by associations that private developers' products fall below the quality and space standards expected in the social rented sector, and will be more costly to maintain in the long run, and this would apply even more to secondhand houses.

Conclusion

Patterns of segregation in England and the wider UK have been set by a combination of spatially uneven economic development and stagnation, by historical approaches to building and rebuilding cities, and by the playing out of tenure restructuring. The evidence in the UK is consistent with global trends: segregation is significant, enduring and more likely to be growing rather than shrinking, and it is most significant in those areas of the country which have suffered from industrial restructuring and lie outwith the recent boom areas in the South and South East. There has been a lot of interest in whether segregation harmfully intensifies disadvantage, and there is still a need for better evidence from England and the UK on neighbourhood effects, but most policy makers and commentators recognise that there is something in the argument.

Hills is right to promote attention to the need to lift more social renting households out of poverty by increasing employment rates. It is questionable though whether this would make a big difference to the concentration of poverty. Many people in social housing lack the human capital to get anything other than low-paid jobs and would be likely to remain poor, albeit in work (see also Robinson, Chapter 7). Like their forebears, those who are economically successful will probably seek to leave social housing. It would have also been useful for Hills to acknowledge the need to do more to balance regional differences in employment, and to recognise the extent to which many tenants in social housing are not, and are not likely to be, in the labour market.

There is also a major dilemma at the heart of this policy area, which is about balancing the task of meeting housing needs with promoting mixed communities. Meeting basic housing needs is still the most convincing rationale for state involvement in housing provision. Hills correctly points out how social housing has downshifted in terms of tenants' social status and incomes over the years. But it is remiss to overlook that, in its heyday, access to council housing was selective, often discriminatory, and did not readily house many of those in the strongest needs (eg, Clapham and Kintrea 1984; Henderson and Karn 1984), a position which was overturned only after a long campaign.

Many of the policy approaches to create mixed communities, instead of welfare housing estates, pose some risk to the prioritisation of needs. In her first week as Housing Minister for England, Caroline Flint floated the notion that new tenants should sign 'commitment contracts' to seek work (BBC 2008). This was interpreted as a regressive workfare proposal to make housing security dependent on getting a job, and is indicative of the direction that the interdependency of employment and social housing policies could take (see Robinson, Chapter 7). Also, unless resources are substantially expanded, the reinvention of social housing for a wide range of income groups is a non-starter as long as needs continue to be prioritised.

Large-scale demolitions and remodelling of estates, however desirable on mixed community grounds, are almost certainly going to have some negative impact on the lives of the some of the poorest citizens, as Cole and Flint (2007) have shown. There is also evidence that appeasement of developers and their private customers in mixed-income new communities has already led to discriminatory, 'selective' lettings. If the concern is to create greater opportunities for the poorest in society, allocation policies which, for example, limit the number of single parent households or households with children in general, or homeless households, potentially undermine the reconnection that mix might bring. They also imply that such households will be disproportionately housed in the old unmixed estates dominated by social housing, perhaps exacerbating their segregation.

Beyond this, the fundamental problem with this whole area of policy is that it is attempting to overturn very longstanding residential choice processes within a housing system that is mainly marketised. Neighbourhoods that offer better amenities (eg, environment, views, public services, schools, transport access, public safety) are in greater demand and cost more. What is more, when they can choose, people select neighbourhoods where other people are similar to themselves (eg, Butler and Robson 2003), because they see advantages in living among others who share their values and represent a social resource. The residential choices of the better-off, where they can be exercised, are mainly about putting as much distance as possible between themselves and the disadvantaged.

Yet, current evidence shows some promise that socially mixed neighbourhoods can be built and can be acceptable to those who have choices to make in the housing market, even if those most easily persuadable are generally not in very elevated positions in the market. Certainly, some newly-built residential areas have a greater social mix than those built in the past, particularly where new social housing is included. In pressured areas of the country the use of the planning system to promote more mixed development has a chance of some minor success. Yet, looking at residential development processes more widely, it certainly does not seem that there is a sure recipe for a new, more integrated pattern of urban development. Even though physical neighbourhood conditions and services have often been improved, sometimes out of all recognition compared to 20 or 30 years ago, council-built estates are still receptacles of poverty. Outside these strongly segregated areas there is a significant task to overcome current patterns of development which tend to reinforce what already exists, and very high land costs make developing subsidised housing for lower-income groups in non-deprived areas hard to stomach in an era of tight public spending. In any case, much of the apparent demand for new social housing in low-demand areas comes from the need to replace obsolete or uneconomic stock.

In spite of these misgivings, there is still a lot to play for. The widespread belief that segregation brings disadvantages, and can at least be tempered by policy, is an important brake on the tendency of labour markets and housing markets to disadvantage people with lower incomes. Longer-term evaluation is needed of current mixed community initiatives, and more attention needs to be given to whether benefits to disadvantaged people living in mixed communities really occur. But, there are already signs that a backlash against mixed communities is beginning. Cheshire (2007) believes that socio-spatial segregation is a positive expression of 'specialist neighbourhoods' which confer benefits on their residents, even for residents of isolated and impoverished estates. It would be disappointing if this kind of free market critique were to overturn the mixed communities policy before it has really got under way.

Keith Kintrea is a Senior Lecturer and Deputy Head of Department at the Department of Urban Studies, University of Glasgow.

References

Atkinson, R., Buck, N. and Kintrea, K., 2005. British neighbourhoods and poverty: linking place and social exclusion. In N. Buck, I. Gordon, A. Harding and I. Turok, eds. Changing cities. Basingstoke: Palgrave Macmillan. Ch.9.

Atkinson, R. and Kintrea, K., 2001. Disentangling neighbourhood effects: evidence from deprived and non-deprived neighbourhoods. Urban Studies, 38(11), p.2277–2298.

Atkinson, R. and Kintrea, K., 2002. Area effects: what do they mean for British housing and regeneration policy? European Journal of Housing Policy, 2(2), p.147–166.

Atkinson, R. and Kintrea, K., 2004. Opportunities and despair, it's all in there: experiences and explanations of area effects and life chances. Sociology, 38(3), p.437–455.

BBC News UK, 2008. 'Work or lose home' says minister. [Internet] 6 May. Available at: http://tinyurl.com/5kwx5s

Bailey, N., Haworth, A., Manzi, T., Paranagamage, P. and Roberts, M., 2006. Creating and sustaining mixed communities: a good practice guide. Coventry: CIH.

Blasius, J., Friedrichs, J. and Galster, G., 2007. Introduction: frontiers of quantifying neighbourhood effects. Housing Studies, 22(5), p.627–636.

Bolster, A., Burgess, S., Johnston, R., Jones, K., Propper, C. and Sarker, R., 2007. Neighbourhoods, households and income dynamics: a semi-parametric investigation of neighbourhood effects. *Journal of Economic Geography,* 7(1), p.1–38.

Bramley, G., Leishman, C., Karley, N., Morgan, J. and Watkins, D., 2007. *Transforming places: housing investment and neighbourhood market change.* York: JRF.

Buck, N., 2001. Identifying neighbourhood effects on social exclusion. *Urban Studies,* 38, p.2251–2275.

Butler, T. and Robson, G., 2003. *London calling: the middle classes and the remaking of Inner London.* London: Berg.

Cheshire, P., 2007. *Segregated neighbourhoods and mixed communities: a critical analysis.* York: JRF.

Clapham, D. and Kintrea, K., 1984. Allocation systems and housing choice. *Urban Studies,* 2(2), p.261–269.

Cole, I. and Flint, J., 2007. *Demolition, relocation and affordable housing: lessons from the housing market renewal pathfinders.* York: JRF and Coventry: CIH.

Crook, T. Currie, J., Jackson, A., Monk, S., Rowley, S., Smith, K. and Whitehead, C., 2002. *Planning gain and affordable housing: making it count.* York: YPS.

DCLG, 2006. *Housing planning policy statement 3.* London: DCLG.

DCLG, 2008. £200m Housing Corporation funding for RSLs to buy stock for affordable housing, London: CLG. [Internet] 2 Jul. Available at: http://tinyurl.com/5w8xtg

Dorling, D., Rigby, J., Wheeler, B., Ballas, D., Thomas, B., Fahmy, E., Gordon, D. and Lupton R., 2007. *Poverty, wealth and place in Britain 1968–2005.* Bristol: Policy Press.

Feinstein, L., Lupton, R., Hammond, C., Mujtaba, T., Salter, E. and Sorhaindo, A., 2008. *The public value of social housing: a longitudinal analysis of the relationship between housing and life chances.* London: Smith Institute.

Fainstein, S., Gordon, I. and Harloe, M., 1992. *Divided cities: New York and London in the contemporary world.* London: Routledge.

Galster, G., 2007. Should policy makers strive for neighbourhood social mix? An analysis of the European evidence base. *Housing Studies,* 22(4), p.523–545.

Galster, G., Marcotte, D., Mandell, M., Wolman, H. and Augustine, N., 2007. The influence of neighbourhood poverty during childhood on fertility, education and earnings outcomes. *Housing Studies,* 22(5), p.723–751.

Henderson, J. and Karn, V., 1984. Race, class and the allocation of public housing in Britain. *Urban Studies,* 21(2), p.115–128.

Hills, J., 2007. *Ends and means: the future of social housing in England.* CASE Report 34, London: CASE and LSE. Available at: http://tinyurl.com/24ms5b

IPPR, 2000. *Housing united: the final report of the IPPR Forum on social housing.* London: IPPR.

Kearns, A. and Mason, P., 2007. Mixed tenure communities and neighbourhood quality. *Housing Studies,* 22(5), p.661–691.

Kintrea, K., 2007. Neighbourhood renewal: recent English experience. *Housing Studies,* 22(2), p.261–282.

Kintrea, K., Bannister, J., Pickering, J., Reid, M. and Suzuki, N., 2008, forthcoming. *Young people and territoriality in British cities.* York: JRF.

Kemeny, J., 1995. *From public housing to the social market: rental policy strategies in comparative perspective.* London: Routledge.

Lupton, R., 2003. *Poverty street.* Bristol: Policy Press.

Lupton, R., 2005. *Changing neighbourhoods? Mapping the geography of poverty and worklessness using the 1991 and 2001 Census.* CASE-Brookings Census Brief 3. London: CASE and LSE.

MacDonald, R. and Marsh, J., 2005. *Disconnected youth?: growing up in Britain's poor neighbourhoods.* Basingstoke: Palgrave Macmillan.

MacDonald. R., Shildrick, T., Webster, C. and Simpson, D., 2005. Growing up in poor neighbourhoods: the significance of class and place in the extended transitions of 'socially excluded' adults. *Sociology,* 39(5), p.873–891.

McCulloch, A., 2001. Ward level deprivation and individual social and economic outcomes in the British Household Panel Survey. *Environment and Planning A,* 33, p.667–684.

Meen, G., Gibb, K., Goody, J., McGrath, T. and Mackinnon, J., 2005. *Economic segregation in England: causes, consequences and policy.* Bristol: Policy Press.

Mingione, E., ed., 1996. *Urban poverty and the underclass.* Oxford: Blackwell.

Noble, M., McLennan, D., Wilkinson, K., Whitworth, A., Barnes, H. and Dibben C., 2008. *The English indices of deprivation.* London: DCLG.

North, D. and Syrett, S., 2006. *The dynamics of local economies and deprived neighbourhoods.* London: DCLG.

Palmer, G., Kenway, P. and Wilcox, S., 2006. *Housing and neighbourhoods monitor.* York: JRF.

Portes, A., 2000. The two meanings of social capital. *Sociological Forum,* 15, p.1–12.

Sassen, S., 2001. *The global city: New York, London, Tokyo.* 2nd ed. Princeton: Princeton University Press.

Silverman, E., Lupton, R. and Fenton, A., 2005. *Mixed and balanced communities: attracting and retaining families in inner city mixed income neighbourhoods.* Coventry: CIH.

Stephens, M., Burns, N. and Mackay, L., 2003. The limits of housing reform: British social housing in a European context. *Urban Studies,* 40(8), p.767–789.

Tunstall, R. and Coulter, A., 2006. *Twenty-five years on twenty estates.* Bristol: Policy Press.

Wilson, W., 1987. *The truly disadvantaged: the inner city, the underclass and public policy.* Chicago: University of Chicago Press.

Chapter 6

Social housing and choice

Hal Pawson

Introduction

In contrast to the way it is organised in some other Northern European countries, British social housing has been characterised as a 'command' system where policy and operational decision-making is primarily administrative rather than market-sensitive (Kemeny 1995). Accordingly, social housing traditions in Britain are deeply imbued with bureaucratic paternalism. Whether agencies of the state or philanthropic, third-sector organisations, social landlords have tended to see their role as to deploy professional expertise or social largesse to act in tenants' interests. For council housing which dominated the field until the 1990s, the traditional view of accountability saw this as entirely achieved through the collective exercise of political choices in the election of local councillors. Part of this was about the conception of council housing as a public service benefiting the whole community, with access based on non-market principles and potentially available to all members of the community as a right of citizenship.

Over the past 20–30 years this traditional conception of public service provision has come under sustained attack from advocates of new forms of citizenship and from those calling for the users of public service users to be treated as active consumers, rather than passive welfare recipients (Clarke 2005). Until recently, most of the running in the social housing field was made by citizenship initiatives aimed at strengthening managerial accountability to tenants in a collective sense. Examples include tenants charters, stock transfer ballots and tenant management co-operatives. Particularly since the election of the New Labour administration in 1997, however, measures to promote tenant choice – as opposed to voice – have tended to take centre stage.

These developments have occurred alongside the evolution of a progressively more residualised social housing sector, a tenure of last resort increasingly occupied only by those with no other choice – albeit, a form of housing offering long-term security. Meanwhile, with the growing affluence enjoyed by the majority of the population, a consumerist culture has arguably become 'the defining spirit of contemporary Britain' (Bramley et al 2004, p.207). Aspects of this include 'the greater role of and belief in markets, the decline of deference, the emphasis on quality, and the fascination with lifestyle and fashion such that 'shopping has become the favourite leisure pursuit' (ibid, p.207).

New Labour's elevation of public service consumerisation to form a key governmental priority in part reflects three main motivations for promoting choice:

* better resource allocation (resulting in improved welfare outcomes)

* a means to drive up management standards, and

* the intrinsic value of choice (choice for its own sake).

This chapter reviews the ways that government policy has sought to promote choice in social housing over the past 25 years, especially since 1997. It begins by outlining the origins of demands for greater choice, before examining the mechanisms used to promote collective forms of choice in social housing. It then addresses government interventions intended to foster individual choice in social housing, focusing, in particular, on choice-based lettings – a model which attempts to adopt a consumerist style of social landlord practice. The discussion considers how choice-based letting works in practice and the extent to which the model actually empowers people seeking social housing, and its advantages and disadvantages from the service user perspective.

Demands for greater choice

As organisations operating largely outside the market, social landlords are not inherently obliged to treat users of their services as consumers whose needs and preferences must drive the business. To the extent that their product is made available at below-market prices, there is little commercial need for landlords to compete for business by sticking close to the customer. Unlike customers in market contexts, existing tenants are far from free to exercise the power of 'exit' – responding to perceived inadequacies in provision by taking their custom elsewhere. Similarly, the legally defined safety net function of social housing has traditionally been seen as emphasising landlords' role as welfare agencies rationing assistance according to needs-related entitlement, rather than being significantly influenced by consumer preferences (Stephens et al 2003).

However, over the past decade, largely through pressure from the Government and regulators, both councils and housing associations have faced growing demands to adopt a more consumerist model. For example, the expectations that landlords will undertake periodic tenants surveys, and be capable of demonstrating how tenant views and preferences have influenced the outcome of best value service reviews. These demands have been promoted mainly through performance criteria, such as the Audit Commission's Key Lines of Enquiry (KLoEs).[1] Failure to adopt such

---

[1] See: http://tinyurl.com/54wt9b

approaches is liable to result in negative inspection ratings, a damaging outcome from a managerial perspective. Ironically, as noted by King (2006), the main dynamic here has a 'top-down' quality, characteristic of Kemeny's command economy, despite the stated objective being to increase tenant influence and choice.

A rationalist justification for such official policies has been the contention that the quality of social landlords' decision-making will be improved where it is informed by the views and preferences of service users. Particularly in New Labour thinking, an allied view has been that the modernisation and legitimisation of public services demands that provider agencies treat service users more as if they were customers in a market context.

Advocacy groups have argued in the same vein. For example, traditional (bureaucratic) approaches to allocating social housing have been criticised as allowing too little scope for applicant choice. In the context of modern consumer society, it has been argued that the opportunity for exercising real choice in the selection of housing should not be denied to social landlords' customers simply because of their reliance on non-market housing (Shelter Scotland 2000). Indeed, it can also be argued that the continued dominance of bureaucratic paternalism in social housing compounds the tenure's stigmatisation as a welfare sector from which residents will aspire to escape if they have the means to do so.

Reflecting similar concerns, the 2000 Housing Green Paper declared an official aspiration to make social housing a tenure of choice (Department of the Environment, Transport and the Regions (DETR) and Department for Work and Pensions (DWP) 2000, para 6.12). Firstly, social housing should become a tenure within which people exercise choice about their housing outcomes. Secondly, a broader cross-section of the public should choose to enter the tenure, in part because of an expectation of being allowed greater freedom to meet their housing preferences. (For a wider discussion on the implications of these ministerial goals see Fitzpatrick and Pawson (2007).)

Collective choice

Since the 1980s, the Government has sought to offer council tenants collective choices around the management of their homes, often through forms of tenant participation. The tenant consultation obligations imposed on local authorities through the Housing Act 1980 marked an important milestone in this process. Subsequently, during the 1990s, further pressure was exerted through the Housing Investment Programme system which incorporated a performance assessment framework where facilitating tenant involvement was a key criterion influencing a council's overall score (and, hence, its housing capital allocation).

Much attention has focused on facilitating scope for choice of landlord. A change of landlord procedure apparently squarely aimed at affording council tenants the power of 'exit' (Hirschman 1970) was the Tenants'

Choice measure introduced in the Housing Act 1988. Presented as a means of enabling dissatisfied tenants to opt out of council control, this was seen by ministers as likely to prove attractive to private landlords wishing to takeon ownership of council estates. And, while the voting system was controversial because of the inclusion of abstentions as votes in favour of change, this was an ambitious device in that it required successor landlords to lease back to the council properties occupied by 'No' voters. In this way, Tenants' Choice attempted to accommodate both individual and collective choices. In practice, however, the scheme proved costly and essentially unworkable – partly because of its necessarily complex mechanics and partly because of the dilemma faced by the Housing Corporation in ensuring that aspirant successor landlords were sufficiently respectable as beneficiaries of the process (Malpass and Mullins 2002). By the time of its repeal in the Housing Act 1996, Tenants' Choice had resulted in the ownership transfer of just 1,470 homes.

Originating at around the same time as Tenants' Choice but, over the long term, much more significant has been the Large Scale Voluntary Transfer regime. Available since 1985, and again according a pivotal role for a tenant ballot, large-scale voluntary transfers in England had resulted in the ownership handover of almost one million former council dwellings by 2007 (Wilcox 2007). With around one-quarter of transfer ballots generating 'No' votes (Munro et al 2005) it is clear that this is more than a purely tokenistic procedure. However, large-scale voluntary transfer proposals are rarely, if ever, tenant-triggered or driven (Mullins et al 1992, 1995; Malpass and Mullins 2002). They can only progress with the agreement of all three key stakeholders – tenants, local authority and central Government – and, even then, only following a long lead-in time. It would be hard to portray the tenant ballot aspect of the large-scale voluntary transfer process as significantly contributing to social housing as a tenure of choice.

Similar comments apply to the collective choice option more recently created for councils to delegate management to arms-length management organisations. As with large-scale voluntary transfers, council tenants certainly have a collective say in the decision, usually through some form of ballot (not all of which have resulted in arms-length management organisation approval). In effect, however, both are processes through which endorsement is sought (by the local authority) rather than choice offered.

Since 2001, the possibility of traditionally-run council housing being switched to large-scale voluntary transfer or arms-length management organisation management has been presented within the context of the official aspiration to bring all social housing up to a specified Decent Homes Standard by 2010 (see Bramley, Chapter 8). Local authorities needing additional funding to achieve Decent Homes Standard compliance have the potential to secure such funding through one of these routes. Official guidance has emphasised that tenant representatives must be involved in the process of defining and appraising the options (Office of the Deputy

Prime Minister (ODPM) 2003a) – another potentially significant arena for the exercise of collective tenant choices.

The right to manage is another legislative tool intended to facilitate collective choice on housing management. Introduced under the Leasehold Reform, Housing and Urban Development Act 1993, this measure enables tenant groups to take on the management of estates while ownership remains with the local authority. Less confrontational than Tenants' Choice, this was nevertheless another mechanism created to satisfy perceived council tenant dissatisfaction with landlord performance. In numerical terms, it has been far more significant than Tenants' Choice, with tenant management organisations responsible for managing over 84,000 homes by 2002 (Mullins and Murie 2006). Importantly, however, the right to manage is available only to council tenants, and not to tenants of housing associations.

Launched in 1999, Tenant Participation Compacts are a more recent vehicle aimed at promoting resident engagement in social housing, intended to facilitate a more genuine spirit of partnership working across the landlord–tenant divide, and generally increasing landlord accountability. However, somewhat in keeping with evaluation findings with respect to other tenant participation structures, evidence for positive impacts of Tenant Participation Compacts on service performance has proved limited (Aldbourne Associates 2003).

Although there has been a recent tendency to focus more on individual choice than on collective voice (see below), the collective tradition remains an active one, as exemplified by the recent establishment of the Tenant Services Authority, a new watchdog body that will, in the words of the official press release, 'crack down on registered social landlords in England who are giving tenants a poor service' (Communities and Local Government (CLG) 2007a). It is envisaged that the new agency, created in response to recommendations from the Cave Review (Cave 2007), will investigate possible breaches of performance standards, with tenants' groups having the power to trigger such inquiries. Also arising from the Cave Review, a National Tenant Voice is being established to ensure that tenant perspectives are incorporated in policy-making at the national level.

Consistent with the view that optimal landlord decision-making requires effective feedback mechanisms, another consumerist theme seen in social housing since the 1980s has been the promotion of market research techniques, such as tenants' surveys, analysis of formal complaints and similar procedures. Since 1997, such activities have been undertaken within the context of the best value regime which has encouraged local authorities and housing associations to undertake periodic service reviews that accord prime significance to the views of both provider staff and service users (ODPM 2003b).

Individual choice

Government aspirations to foster greater individual choice for social sector tenants are also far from new. However, in the 1980s and 1990s, these focused largely on facilitating the ability of council tenants to exit the tenure in favour of home ownership. While, by 2006, 1.8 million council tenants in England had taken up their right to buy established in the Housing Act 1980, this choice is, of course, available now only to that small minority of better-off tenants able to raise the purchase price.[2] Also, somewhat paradoxically, it can be argued that 'the greatest constraint to user choice in social housing [has been] the progressive sale of the best quality homes and failure to invest adequately in either new homes or enhancement of remaining stock' (Mullins and Murie 2006, p.221).

While the right to buy remains operational, restrictions on terms of sale (both in terms of eligibility and discount entitlement) (Murie and Jones 2006) have seen transactions falling markedly in recent years. In the three years to 2006/07, total sales in England dropped more than 75 per cent to just 16,896 (CLG 2007b). This is significantly below the Housing Corporation's annual target number of new social housing approvals – 24,500 for 2007/08. Post-1997, ministerial promotion of individual choice in the social sector has been less centrally concerned with facilitating exit from council housing. Instead it has focused on promoting a more consumerist approach to the management of social housing where landlords seek to offer more personalised services (Cabinet Office 2006). This is presented as empowering tenants and others seeking to enter social housing, although many commentators have characterised such moves as more concerned with 'responsibilisation' as an advanced liberal approach to governance (Clarke 2005; Cowan and McDermont 2006). In social housing this form of public service modernisation has been exemplified mainly through the introduction of choice-based lettings.

Traditionally, the process of letting social tenancies has involved people seeking tenancies (house-seekers) registering on a landlord's waiting list and being invited at this stage to indicate their housing preferences – for example, on property type and area. Applicants must also often provide extensive detail on their current housing and personal circumstances to inform their housing needs assessment. Each needs factor is generally represented by a points value so that the applicant's priority is determined by their cumulative points score in relation to the points scores of other registered applicants (Pawson et al 2001).

---

[2] By 2006/07 the average discounted price paid by right to buy purchasers in England had risen to £67,795 – CLG, *Housing Statistics Live Tables*, Table 643. Available at: http://tinyurl.com/6d7az4 This implies that tenants without significant savings would need household incomes of at least £20,000 to make purchase affordable. As at 2004/05, however, only 18 per cent of council tenants were in receipt of such incomes – CLG, *Survey of English Housing Live Tables*, Table S114. Available at: http://tinyurl.com/5wq5qs

Allocating vacant properties under this system involves a staff member matching the details of an available-to-let dwelling with those of highly ranked house-seekers. Therefore, the official has to interpret each relevant house-seeker's recorded preferences and also to assume that these remain valid (despite having been specified some time previously). The selected applicant – who may have been awaiting a tenancy offer for a prolonged period – is presented with a simple choice of whether to accept or reject the offer of a property considered appropriate by the organisation.

House-seekers, under this model, play a largely passive role. And, with thecritical function of matching property and applicant in the hands of a housing officer, rather than the applicant, an unsuitable allocation is arguably more likely than if the applicant had played a direct role in the process. Consequently, there will be an increased risk of dissatisfaction with the outcome, both because choice has intrinsic value to the house-seeker and because the result is less likely to be optimal in objective terms with respect to the match between applicant needs/preferences and property features/location. A knock-on effect will be to increase the likelihood of tenancies being given up prematurely, with resulting financial costs to the landlord and social, as well as financial, costs to the tenant.

Choice-based letting schemes originated in the Netherlands (where it is known as the 'supply model'). Spreading throughout Dutch social housing during the 1990s (Kullberg 1997, 2002), they involve the introduction of transparency through the open advertising of available-to-let vacancies. People seeking social housing can view and bid for properties seen as suitable. Therefore, in matching house-seekers and vacancies, the onus switches from landlord to house-seeker. However, the landlord retains the responsibility for ranking competing bids for each advertised property, applying local rationing rules to determine the bidder with greatest priority and, hence, the individual likely to be offered the tenancy. Choice-based letting schemes usually operate on the basis of a predictable lettings cycle where available-to-let vacancies are advertised periodically (eg, weekly or fortnightly).

Another important principle of choice-based lettings is that lettings outcomes are published. This is both in the interests of accountability and intended to help inform decisions by other house-seekers by indicating the level of priority required to secure a property of a given type in a given place (Brown et al 2000). Typically, choice-based letting landlords list recent lettings on their website and/or in press advertising, showing basic details of the properties concerned and the priority level of the successful applicant (eg, number of rehousing points, priority band and application date).

Characterising choice-based lettings as a form of choice without competition, the Audit Commission sees it as potentially beneficial in producing 'more flexibility and greater personalisation for users' as well as helping 'to match limited supply with demand better' (Audit Commission 2006, p.5). As argued by Marsh (2004, p.189):

'At one extreme, better market information [under choice-based lettings] could lead some applicants to realise that the amount of currency they possess will be insufficient to access social housing locally. At the other extreme, in areas of low demand, it could demonstrate to households who erroneously believed social housing was available only to those in need that they may have a chance to access a property.'

This is consistent with the Hills comment that choice-based letting has the potential to empower house-seekers, at least 'at the margin' (Hills 2007, p.20).

Hills (2007) reminds us that here, as for any commodity made available at a controlled, sub-market price, some form of administrative allocation is inherently required to accommodate excess demand. Rationing rules are substituted for purchasing power and these mean that consumer choice is inevitably constrained. The need for such rules means that the social landlord gatekeeper role remains inherent (Cowan and Marsh 2005). Moreover, the longstanding legal framework for rationing has continued unchanged, irrespective of ministers' professed enthusiasm for a quasi-market style process. While they are exhorted to simplify and make more transparent their administrative rules (DETR and Department of Health (DoH) 2000), landlords are still required to prioritise applicants, mainly in relation to assessed housing need (CLG 2007c).

Making a similar point, Marsh (2004) notes that social landlords retain substantial control, even under choice-based letting schemes, through their role in setting the rules of the game. Not only do they fix the overall bidder ranking rules (see above), but they also determine eligibility. This involves judging who is qualified to bid, both in general terms and in relation to specific properties where detailed labelling restrictions are sometimes imposed in an effort to shape aggregate housing outcomes. Consequently, as Marsh sees it, 'the consumer is in no way dominant' under the choice-based letting model (ibid, p.194).

However, while recognising the inherent limitations, Hills nevertheless saw some scope for a more consumerist approach to social landlord lettings and welcomed choice-based letting schemes as a means of improving outcomes, at least at the margin. And, as demonstrated by research evidence, choice-based letting has achieved modest success with respect to stated official objectives. The main source of evidence from which the following findings are drawn is the official longer-term impact of choice-based letting study (Pawson et al 2006) – hereafter 'the 2006 research'. This concluded that choice-based lettings tended to enhance tenancy sustainment, albeit by only a limited extent. Drawing on data for 15 schemes in different parts of Britain, it was found that the proportion of tenants giving up new tenancies within 12 months typically fell by 10–20 per cent following the introduction of choice-based letting schemes.

Similarly, the study found that the small number of cross-borough choice-based letting schemes seeking to promote inter-authority moves had achieved some success in this respect. Nevertheless, there was no clear sign that choice-based lettings had generally led to increased cross-boundary moves. The evidence on whether choice-based letting schemes enhance spatial mobility at an intra-authority level is somewhat mixed. Typical distances moved by transfer applicants in one London borough fell slightly under choice-based letting schemes. In two northern cities, however, typical distances moved by new tenants increased by at least 50 per cent under the new system, apparently validating the hypothesis that choice-based letting should facilitate increased intra-area mobility because applicants are encouraged – by viewing advertisements for available-to-let properties – to consider the possibility of a move outside their existing home area (and other known areas previously seen as acceptable).

Choice-based lettings seek to encourage housing applicants to trade-off various housing preferences – eg, to consider bidding for a property in a previously unfamiliar or less popular area in order to secure a tenancy offer more quickly. As schemes bed down and become more familiar there is evidence, albeit indirect, of applicants responding accordingly. Hence, the 2006 research identified a tendency for average numbers of bids to grow faster in initially less popular areas than in initially more popular areas. This confirms the social landlord view that choice-based lettings can be effective in generating additional demand for vacancies in previously problematic areas. However, other research evidence suggests that most existing tenants are fairly resistant to the notion of playing-off area preference against other factors (eg lower rents) (Walker et al 2002). Similarly, the 2006 research found that, for many applicants, area was the most important factor in their bids, and the factor they were least likely to compromise on (see also Monk et al, Chapter 9). These findings emphasise the need to avoid overstating the extent to which choice-based lettings may facilitate the widening of house-seeker choices prompted by being made aware of available properties in areas previously unconsidered.

There is little evidence of demand responsiveness to overall shortage under choice-based letting schemes. According to the theory, people seeking tenancies in more pressured areas but who have relatively little priority should become aware of this through observing the priority status of those recently housed in comparison to their own ranking. This would suggest that, following an initial increase, the number of active bidders following the introduction of choice-based lettings would fairly quickly peak, as those more lowly ranked come to appreciate their poor prospects of success and, hence, cease to participate. In practice, such a pattern was found in only one of the four schemes from which it proved possible to obtain data in the 2006 research. These findings sow doubts as to whether feedback information (lettings results) routinely provided under most choice-based letting schemes is, in fact, understood as the quasi-market theorists suggest should be the case.

To the extent that it has provoked controversy, much of the scepticism expressed about choice-based letting as a concept has stemmed from concerns that it could disadvantage certain groups – in particular, those with serious and/or urgent needs, and certain vulnerable groups less capable of engaging with the quasi-market system.

One set of anxieties has surrounded the possibility that choice-based lettings could benefit waiting list and transfer list applicants, to the detriment of households rehoused as statutorily homeless (see Fitzpatrick, Chapter 3). Shelter research focusing on some early choice-based letting schemes found that 'homeless applicants have less choice, and are forced to bid more often or more quickly for properties than other applicants' (Grannum 2005, p.2). As a result, there was a concern that choice-based lettings could 'result in increasing concentrations of previously homeless households in low-demand areas' (ibid, p.2).

In practice, however, the 2006 research found that landlords operating choice-based letting schemes had configured their rules and procedures so that statutorily homeless households were somewhat *less likely* to be housed in less popular areas than under pre-choice-based letting arrangements. It might be assumed that this has been achieved simply by increasing the chances of homeless households being housed in average popularity areas, but evidence shows that choice-based letting had increased the propensity for formerly homeless households to be accommodated in high-demand neighbourhoods. Importantly, the research also confirmed that only a small number of landlords running choice-based letting schemes had opted to exclude homeless households from the system (ie continuing to allocate properties to this group under the traditional administrative approach).

A distinct set of concerns about the potentially negative impacts of choice-based lettings relates to vulnerable people more generally. Compared with the traditional allocations model, choice-based letting requires a more active engagement with the process on the part of house-seekers. Within the generally fairly deprived cohort of people seeking to enter social housing, certain groups could be particularly at risk because of their limited capacity to play the active consumer role that the system demands. Key examples would include:

- very elderly or infirm people
- people with learning difficulties
- people with visual impairment or a lack of literacy, and
- recent migrants and others without a good command of English.

The 2006 research found that most social landlords operating choice-based letting schemes appreciated the need for special measures to protect the interests of vulnerable groups at risk of being disadvantaged by the active engagement required under the system. Commonly, such measures include the maintenance of an assisted list of house-seekers eligible for special help. Assisted list members receive, by direct mail, information on available-to-let vacancies and how to bid for these. Under many choice-based letting schemes, such information is also routinely disseminated to advocacy organisations and/or made available in minority languages, British Sign Language, audio and large font formats. Making property information available by telephone, another technique often employed, is a potentially important facility for people with sight impairment or lack of literacy.

Most choice-based letting schemes devote some staffing resources to directly advising and assisting applicants on how to bid and what to bid for. Perhaps of equal importance are programmes widely run to coincide with the introduction of choice-based letting to inform and train local caring professionals and advocates on how the system works, and on how to advise and assist clients seeking housing, such as through making proxy bids on their behalf.

The extent to which techniques of these kinds succeed in protecting the interests of key vulnerable groups is, unfortunately, very difficult to determine – especially given the typical absence of relevant monitoring activity by choice-based letting landlords (CLG 2009 (forthcoming)). However, while recognising that choice-based lettings' delegation of greater responsibility to house-seekers entails risks for such groups, it should also be recognised that opening up lettings in this way can be highly beneficial to certain vulnerable households through facilitating the active involvement of family members and other advocates (eg case workers, specialist advice agencies) in ways which were impossible under traditional closed allocations systems.

A wider anxiety about choice-based letting schemes expressed by some commentators (eg, Grannum 2005) has been the worry that an emphasis on system transparency and the legitimacy of system outcomes could be in conflict with equity objectives – and, indeed, with local authorities' legal obligations embodied in the Housing Act 1996 reasonable preference criteria. The hypothesis here is that systems according greater priority to those with the ability to wait (because their housing conditions are tolerable) will inevitably disadvantage those with urgent needs. Consequently, much debate has focused on the housing prioritisation criteria incorporated within choice-based letting schemes, and the balance struck between assessed need and waiting time.

Apparently consistent with such concerns, recent survey work for CLG undertaken by the author and focusing on housing allocations systems operated in two regions of England revealed that, as perceived by local authority housing staff, the significance of waiting time tended to be much greater under choice-based lettings than under traditional allocations schemes. Whereas respondents in 19 of the 20 choice-based letting authorities (95 per cent) considered waiting time to be 'quite significant' or 'very significant' in contributing to an applicant's housing priority, this was true for only seven (22 per cent) of the other 32 authorities.

Nevertheless, statistical evidence from CORE (data on social landlord lettings) provides no evidence for the hypothesis that, under choice-based letting schemes, those in serious housing need are being 'squeezed out' by people with priority largely based on waiting time. Analysis of 2006/07 lettings by the 54 stock transfer housing associations operating choice-based letting schemes in England found that the proportion of lettings to households *not entitled* to reasonable preference was identical to that recorded by their non-choice-based letting counterpart landlords. Therefore, at least in quantitative terms, there is no evidence that switching to a choice-based letting is liable to produce a pattern of housing outcomes less consistent with legislative obligations than previously achieved. While the 2006 research attempted to go further than this by examining choice-based letting's impact on the pattern of lettings in terms of quality/desirability (and found no cause for concern), there is scope for such analysis to be repeated in the future.

Although the 2006 research paints a broadly positive picture about the longer-term impacts of choice-based lettings it raised some questions about the 'received wisdom' that the system is overwhelmingly popular with housing applicants. Many of those questioned in the research saw choice-based letting bidding as a positive, pro-active way of looking for housing. However, some who had been bidding unsuccessfully over long periods of time found the system frustrating and lacked confidence in its fairness. An important factor here is that, while choice-based letting is sometimes presented as being inherently transparent, many bidders remained confused about applicant-ranking rules. In part, this probably reflects the fact that on their websites and elsewhere many landlords focus on explaining bidding rules and procedures while tending to play down their bidder prioritisation criteria. Scottish research on choice-based letting applicant perspectives also raises doubts about the model's transparency (Dudleston and Harkins 2007).

That many people seeking to access social housing through choice-based letting schemes find this an unrewarding experience is not surprising given the very large numbers of bids typically recorded for each advertised property. The 2006 research showed that average bids per let exceeded 50 in several case study areas, and there have been reports of adverts drawing more than 500 applications (see, for example, Edinburgh Evening News 2007a). In part, this simply reflects the large imbalance between demand and supply for social housing which exists in most parts of the country (see Bramley, Chapter 8). With the spread of choice-based lettings having coincided with the tightening of the housing market over the past few years, some have concluded that choice-based letting has, in itself, reduced social housing supply. To the extent that it achieves its aim of reducing subsequent tenancy turnover, there could be an element of truth in this. Taking this a step further, however, it could also be argued that contracting turnover in social housing may well contribute to reduced demand, to the extent that some of those seeking housing are people who have failed to sustain tenancies, and bearing in mind that choice-based letting could help to minimise such events.

Under the 'banded' priority frameworks adopted by many choice-based letting schemes it is often the case that only a very small proportion of lettings are made to bidders classed outside the high needs bands. For example, in one London borough covered by the 2006 research over 99 per cent of all lets in 2004/05 were to applicants in the top three (of four) needs-related bands within which applicants were designated. While the fourth band – those assessed as having no housing need – contained 37 per cent of all applicants, lets to group members accounted for less than one per cent of total lets. In another scheme operated in a rural area of southern England, 86 per cent of 2004/05 lets were to 'Emergency' or 'Gold Band' applicants, and only two per cent were to 'Bronze Band' applicants (the quarter of all registered applicants classed as 'low need/no need' cases). In a northern city case study, however, there was a rather different picture, with 'non-priority' applicants (70 per cent of total registered applicants) accounting for 50 per cent of lettings.

Therefore, for many people without assessed housing need but living in high-demand areas, participation in choice-based letting is unlikely to be perceived as providing much in the way of real choice.[3] Although it is clearly illogical to imagine that the administrative switch to choice-based letting will, of itself, increase social housing supply, opening up the lettings process via publicly accessible advertising may well have the effect of unjustifiably raising expectations for large numbers of people. And, while it is strongly discouraged in official guidance (CLG 2007b), there could be a coherent case (in high demand areas) for running choice-based lettings as a closed system where the dissemination of information on available-to-let vacancies is restricted to those above a given priority threshold. Alternatively, or in addition, official guidance should place greater emphasis on the need to inform and counsel low-priority applicants of their realistic chances of securing a tenancy under choice-based letting schemes.

Among those with high priority status it seems more likely that choice-based letting will often be perceived as offering a degree of real choice. Even so, many such households will find themselves needing to bid repeatedly before being successful in receiving a tenancy offer. Also, as revealed by the 2006 research, it needs to be recognised that statutorily homeless households are often subject to much more constrained choice-based letting choices than other applicants – in this sense retaining some similarity with traditional allocations systems where homeless applicants are often entitled to one offer only while others have more. For example, they may be subject to bidding time-limits which mean that, failing their having made a

---

[3] Witness the case of the shop assistant facing retirement and concerned at the high cost of his privately rented flat. Thanks to being designated as 'low priority' under the City of Edinburgh Council choice-based letting scheme, this tenant reportedly made 370 unsuccessful bids for council tenancies over a three-year period up to 2007 (Edinburgh Evening News 2007b).

successful bid during the relevant period, they will be required to accept a tenancy offer generated in the traditional 'top down' manner. As shown above, however, this does not, in practice, appear to result in typically worse housing outcomes for the statutorily homeless group than in the pre-choice-based letting era. This may be because, with local authorities facing an imperative to house such households as fast as possible (thereby minimising temporary accommodation costs), they benefit from more help (active case management) from social landlord staff.

So, to sum up on choice-based letting, the research evidence suggests that such systems are, in the UK context, substantially managed markets, that they can be configured to minimise risks with respect to equity, and that they can generate at least modest benefits in terms of user empowerment and satisfaction (as reflected by subsequently improved tenancy sustainment). However, there is a danger of choice-based letting systems being shaped too much by landlords' managerial priorities and a risk of the housing profession sinking into a complacent and misplaced assumption that transparency objectives have been fully realised. In a radical critique, aimed at more fully realising choice-based letting objectives, Leunig (2008) advocates individual social housing tenants having the right to trigger the open market sale of their homes, with the proceeds being used (by their landlord) to purchase a home the tenant would prefer. As well as enabling tenant choice, this would facilitate mixed-tenure communities. While the practicality of such a scheme is highly questionable in terms of its asset-management implications, the idea perhaps helps to emphasise choice-based letting schemes' limitations as a consumer empowerment device.

Conclusion

While attracting less media attention than education and health, social housing has been a key site of action in New Labour's crusade for consumerised public services. In the main, this has been expressed through a strong ministerial push for choice-based letting as a quasi-market approach to housing management. Research suggests that choice-based letting has achieved key official objectives, albeit in a generally modest way. At the same time, there is no evidence to substantiate concerns that choice-based letting might systematically compound existing patterns of disadvantage. However, partly reflecting the need to accommodate the model within the prevailing social and economic context, it is clear that choice-based letting, as operated in the UK, generally involves highly managed and rule-bound systems.

Choice-based letting schemes, as the flagship New Labour policy in this area, can be depicted as an element of a larger body of reforms aimed at transforming Britain's social rented sector from a command system to a social market (Stephens et al 2003). While preserving a framework where housing is let at below market rents, such a model would involve housing associations as the prime landlord type, 'using pricing structures to register consumer preferences and choices' (ibid, p.768).

However, while it may function effectively in countries such as the Netherlands, Stephens et al argue that it could be mistaken to assume that a social market framework can be unproblematically imported and implemented in the British context. As their research demonstrates, Britain's social rented sector is far more associated with poverty than is true of comparable European countries. This, in turn, reflects the proportionately greater incidence of poverty seen in Britain. Almost one-fifth of UK households (19 per cent) were at risk of poverty in 1999, in terms of receiving incomes below 60 per cent of the UK median value (Dennis and Guio 2003). This compares with the EU15–wide average value of 15 per cent. Among EU15 member states, only Portugal and Greece recorded higher poverty rates on this measure.

Within this context, the primary safety net role of Britain's social rented sector can be seen as entirely logical. However, the scope for British councils and housing associations to accommodate middle-income (or 'no housing need') households is consequently far less than for their counterpart agencies elsewhere in Northern Europe. This is an important factor limiting the scope for a highly marketised approach where need ceases to be the prime determinant of housing priority.

For people priced out of home ownership the attraction of a social tenancy is not, of course, only a matter of sub-market rents. Since the deregulation of private renting in 1988, whereas security of tenure has been available to tenants of councils and housing associations, few new private tenancies have offered such a benefit. Removing such security, as has recently been advocated by some commentators, would surely conflict with aspirations for social housing as a tenure of choice – both because households are less likely to choose to enter the tenure, and are also prevented from exercising the choice to stay in it.

Hal Pawson is Professorial Fellow at the School of the Built Environment, Heriot-Watt University, Edinburgh.

References

Audit Commission, 2006. *Choosing well: analysing the costs and benefits of choice in local public services.* Available at: http://tinyurl.com/5gwn77

Aldbourne Associates, 2003. *Interim evaluation of tenant participation compacts.* London: ODPM. Available at: http://tinyurl.com/68rb7v

Bramley, G., Munro, M. and Pawson, H., 2004. *Key issues in housing: policies and markets in 21st century Britain.* Basingstoke: Palgrave.

Brown, T., Hunt, R. and Yates, N., 2000. *Lettings: a question of choice.* Coventry: CIH.

Cabinet Office, 2006. *The UK Government's approach to public service reform: a discussion paper.* London: Cabinet Office. Available at: http://tinyurl.com/6x4zuw

Cave, M., 2007. *Every tenant matters: a review of social housing regulation.* London: CLG. Available at: http://tinyurl.com/5n2m6x

Clarke, J., 2005. New Labour's citizens: activated, empowered, responsibilised, abandoned? *Critical Social Policy,* 25(4), p.447–463.

CLG, 2007a. New steps for new social housing watchdog, 15 Oct. Available at: http://tinyurl.com/5de2k4

CLG, 2007b. *Housing Statistics Live Tables,* Table 670. Available at: http://tinyurl.com/5ts27j

CLG, 2007c. *Allocation of accommodation: choice-based lettings: code of guidance for local housing authorities (consultation draft).* London: CLG. Available at: http://tinyurl.com/5cakxb

CLG, 2009 (forthcoming). *Empowering the participation of vulnerable groups in choice-based lettings – a good practice guide.* London: CLG.

Cowan, D. and Marsh, A., 2005. From need to choice, welfarism to advanced liberalism? Problematics of social housing allocation. *Legal Studies,* 25(1), p.22–48.

Cowan, D. and McDermont, M., 2006. *Regulating social housing: governing decline.* Abingdon: Routledge-Cavendish.

Dennis, I. and Guio, A.C., 2003. *Poverty and social exclusion in the EU after Laeken – part 1: statistics in focus: population and social conditions.* Luxembourg: Eurostat. Available at: http://tinyurl.com/6bag78

DETR and DoH, 2000. *Quality and choice: a decent home for all – the Housing Green Paper.* London: DETR. Available at: http://tinyurl.com/6zwwld

Dudleston, A. and Harkins, J., 2007. *Improving access and maximising choice: the applicants' perspective on allocation systems.* Edinburgh: Scottish Executive. Available at: http://tinyurl.com/55j4yo

Edinburgh Evening News, 2007a. One home, 720 bids. Edinburgh Evening News, 27 Mar. Available at: http://tinyurl.com/5msucp

Edinburgh Evening News, 2007b. 370 bids in three years and no closer to a council home. Edinburgh Evening News, 10 Apr. Available at: http://tinyurl.com/5qs7bd

Fitzpatrick, S. and Pawson, H., 2007. Welfare safety net or tenure of choice? The dilemma facing social housing policy in England. *Housing Studies,* 22(2), p.163–182.

Grannum, C., 2005. *A question of choice.* London: Shelter.

Hills, J., 2007. *Ends and means: the future roles of social housing in England.*CASE Report 34. London: CASE and LSE. Available at: http://tinyurl.com/24ms5b

Hirschman, A.O., 1970. *Exit, voice, and loyalty: responses to decline in firms, organizations, and states.* Cambridge, MA: Harvard University Press.

Kemeny, J., 1995. *From public housing to the social market: rental policy strategies in comparative perspective.* London: Routledge.

King, P., 2006. *Choice and the end of social housing.* London: Institute for Economic Affairs.

Kullberg, J., 1997. From waiting lists to adverts: the allocation of social rental dwellings in the Netherlands. *Housing Studies,* 12(3), p.393–403.

Kullberg, J., 2002. Consumers' response to choice based letting mechanisms. *Housing Studies,* 17(4), p.549–579.

Leunig, T., 2008. An equal footing. Inside Housing. 13 Jun, p.22.

Malpass, P. and Mullins, D., 2002. Local authority housing stock transfer in the UK: from local initiative to national policy. *Housing Studies,* 17(4), p.673–686.

Marsh, A., 2004. The inexorable rise of the rational consumer? The Blair government and the reshaping of social housing. *European Journal of Housing Policy,* 4(2), p.185–207.

Mullins, D. and Murie, A., 2006. *Housing policy in the UK.* Basingstoke: Palgrave.

Mullins, D., Niner, P. and Riseborough, M., 1992. *Evaluating large scale voluntary transfers of local authority housing – interim report.* London: HMSO.

Mullins, D., Niner, P. and Riseborough, M., 1995. *Evaluating large scale voluntary transfers of local authority housing.* London: HMSO.

Munro, M., Pawson, H. and Monk, S. 2005. *Evaluation of English housing policy 1975–2000: theme 4 – widening choice.* Available at: http://tinyurl.com/5teuqz

Murie A. and Jones, C., 2006. *The right to buy: analysis and evaluation of a housing policy.* Blackwell: Oxford.

ODPM, 2003a. *Delivering decent homes: option appraisal – guidance for local authorities.* Available at: http://tinyurl.com/5hjz2t

ODPM, 2003b. *Best value in housing and homelessness framework.* London: ODPM. Available at: http://tinyurl.com/646xtd

Pawson, H., Levison, D., Lawton, G., Third, H. and Parker J., 2001. *Local authority policy and practice on allocations, transfers and homelessness.* London: DETR.

Pawson, H., Jones, C., Watkins, D., Donohoe, T., Netto, G., Fancy, C., Clegg, S. and Thomas A., 2006. *Monitoring the longer term impact of choice-based lettings.* London: DCLG. Available at: http://tinyurl.com/67x85w

Shelter Scotland, 2000. *Briefing on allocations policies.* Edinburgh: Shelter Scotland.

Stephens, M., Burns, N. and MacKay, L., 2003. The limit of housing reform: British social rented housing in a European context. *Urban Studies,* 40(4), p.767–789.

Walker, B., Marsh, A., Wardman, M. and Niner, P., 2002. Modelling tenants' choices in the public rented sector: a stated preference approach. *Urban Studies,* 39(4), p.665–688.

Wilcox, S. 2007. *UK housing review 2007/08.* Coventry and London: CIH and Building Societies Association.

Chapter 7

Social housing and worklessness

David Robinson

Introduction

The last decade has witnessed a steady rise in the number of people in employment in the UK and a fall in unemployment. However, these developments in the labour market have not benefited all groups and communities equally. The result is the growing concentration of unemployment and economic inactivity (together referred to as 'worklessness') in particular sections of society. This concentrating effect has been revealed to have a spatial dimension, analysis pointing to places where a relatively large proportion of the population are out of work and on benefits (Social Exclusion Unit (SEU) 2004). Consistent with the increasing segregation and polarisation of Britain along lines of poverty and wealth (Dorling et al 2007), this emerging geography of worklessness has been recognised as a cause for concern by the Government, and efforts to tackle worklessness have increasingly focused on specific groups and neighbourhoods. Within this context, particular attention has been paid to areas of social housing and the situation of social tenants.

In his recent review of the future role of social housing, John Hills observed that, in 2006, despite accounting for less than 20 per cent of the national housing stock, nearly one-third of 9.1 million workless people in England were resident in the social rented sector and that the worklessness rate in the sector was nearly twice that in the private rented sector (Hills 2007). This situation reflects the rise in levels of worklessness within the social rented sector over the last 25 years. In 1981, the head of household was not in work in half of all households in the sector. By 2007, according to the Labour Force Survey, this figure had risen to two-thirds. Over the last ten years, there has also been an increase in the proportion of households where all members are economically inactive, reflecting the role that the social rented sector now plays in accommodating a relatively large proportion of long-term sick and disabled people. In 2005, 45 per cent of working-age council tenants and 43 per cent of working age housing association tenants were economically inactive (Cannizzaro and Percival 2006).

The obvious response to this evidence is to point out that access and choice within the private housing market is determined by income and wealth, which in turn is closely associated with labour market position.

People disadvantaged in the labour market can, therefore, often struggle to secure and maintain a place in the private sector. In response, many turn to the social rented sector, which has been reconstituted over the last 20 years to serve as a safety net tenure for people in housing need. Relatively high levels of worklessness are therefore to be expected among social tenants. Hills (2007) recognises this point, noting that the profile of social tenants has changed over the last 20 years, with an increasing proportion displaying characteristics that are generally associated with a weak position in the labour market, including high rates of disability or long-term sickness, lone parenthood, and people from a minority ethnic background. However, he goes on to point to in-house analysis by the Department for Work and Pensions (DWP) found that:

'... where a social tenant is affected by one such disadvantage, their rate of worklessness is much higher than for those with the same disadvantage (although not necessarily to the same degree) who do not live in social housing.... [and].... for any given number of overlapping disadvantages, those in social housing have lower employment rates.' (Hills 2007, p.100–102.)

Hills suggests that this finding is all the more concerning given the work-related incentives presumed to be associated with living in social housing, including sub-market rents and security of tenure.

This analysis prompts the question of whether there is something intrinsic about social housing that inhibits labour market engagement. The DWP research referenced by Hills concludes that levels of worklessness within the social rented sector cannot be fully explained by the (observable) characteristics of the people who live within it (Cannizzaro and Percival 2006). Policy has been less reserved in its judgement, concluding that being a social rented tenant is an independent predictor of worklessness, and has set about reforming and refocusing housing management in a bid to reduce the inhibiting effect that living in the sector is presumed to have on labour market engagement and to boost levels of working across the tenant base.

This chapter considers the logic underpinning this agenda. Discussion begins by outlining the recent policy initiatives and proposals directed at addressing the relatively high levels of worklessness in the social rented sector, and considering the rationales informing these developments. The validity of these assumptions, and the viability of the proposed response, are then critically questioned by drawing on findings from a recent major study exploring the links between social housing and worklessness.

Social tenants and worklessness: the policy agenda

Policy-makers appear convinced that there is a link between social housing and worklessness, above and beyond the fact that the role of the sector within the housing system inevitably results in the over-representation, within the tenant base, of vulnerable groups who are disadvantaged in the labour market. Employment rates in the sector are reported to have collapsed (Flint 2008a) and large estates of social housing – characterised as pockets of low employment and low aspiration (Communities and Local Government (CLG) and DWP 2007) – have been identified as the source of the problem. Referring to the culture of 'no one works around here', the Minister for Housing has argued that social housing has the potential to act as a deterrent to work because it exposes people to concentrations of unemployment and poverty, asserting that:

'... if you are in a family, an estate, a neighbourhood where nobody works that impacts on your own aspiration. It is a form of peer pressure.' (Flint, quoted in *The Guardian*, 5 February 2008.)

In response, the policy challenge has been identified as reconstituting these neighbourhoods in a bid to promote greater diversity:

'Originally, council housing brought together people from different social backgrounds and professions but this has declined. We need to think radically and start a national debate about how we can reverse this trend, to build strong, diverse estates.' (Flint 2008a.)

This diagnosis taps into cultural explanations of worklessness that have increasingly informed UK labour market policy. At their heart, is the assumption that concentrated areas of worklessness (including social housing estates) represent segregated communities that nurture cultures which assert values at odds with the work ethic and undermine participation in paid employment, thereby restricting access to associated opportunities (see also Kintrea, Chapter 5). This conviction lies at the heart of the government's national strategy to achieve full employment:

'... the highest concentrations of worklessness occur in very small areas. A "culture of worklessness" or "poverty of aspirations" can develop in such areas, generating a vicious and self-perpetuating cycle leading not only to high levels of worklessness but also to crime, deprivation, and social exclusion. It is important that these cycles are broken and these concentrations addressed.' (HM Treasury and DWP 2002, p.50.)

Following this logic, the challenge becomes reconstituting local communities – in this case social housing estates – to promote cultural change. Housing policy is pursuing this objective in two particular ways.

The first approach might be described as 'exogenous change' or 'change from outside', and focuses on securing a transformation in the local attitudes and outlook by promoting population change. This approach is rooted in the mixed communities agenda, which associates (predominantly) single tenure estates in deprived areas with social problems. In response, policy is actively promoting both the redevelopment of existing estates and the development of new areas of housing in a bid to ensure the provision of a mix of housing of different types and tenures and, thereby, the settlement of a wide range of households of different sizes, ages and incomes within neighbourhoods (Cooper 2007). This thinking, clearly evident in the Minister for Housing's call for the creation of more diverse estates, relies for its legitimacy on the assumption that residential integration leads to social interaction between different groups and cultures. In relation to worklessness, it is assumed that greater social mix results in workless tenants 'rubbing shoulders' with people in work and, through this contact, acquiring a more positive disposition to work (see also Kintrea, Chapter 5).

The second approach to promoting a cultural shift in the attitudes of social tenants toward formal paid work might be described as the pursuit of 'endogenous change' or 'change from within' and focuses on challenging indigenous cultures through interventions targeted at existing residents. It is possible to discern two emerging approaches to promoting change from within contemporary housing policy. The first, which might be labelled the therapeutic, focuses on providing social tenants with advice, support and assistance to facilitate movement into work. Arguing that there are many unemployed people who could find work with the right training and support, the Minister for Housing has identified social landlords as having a key role to play in tackling worklessness:

> 'They know their tenants. They are also often trusted by their tenants when other services are viewed with suspicion. They can put this knowledge, this positive relationship, to good use, by working with other services to help their tenants find the training or work they need. And already, of course, many are already doing this... The challenge is to make sure that it happens more widely.' (Flint 2008a.)

To this end, particular attention has focused on integrating housing and employment and training advice. The Government is sponsoring five local partnerships, involving local authorities, social landlords and employment agencies, to develop new approaches to promoting advice on housing options alongside employment and training advice (Cooper 2007). An extension of housing options services has also been proposed, beyond the original focus on the provision of advice about local housing opportunities and options for people at risk of homelessness (see Fitzpatrick, Chapter 3), to provide advice relevant to people's overall circumstances, including advice on childcare, training and employment (Flint 2008b).

These initiatives reflect the supply-side orthodoxy that has characterised labour market policy in recent years. Accepting that 'work pays for all', as Freud (2007) asserted in his review of the government's Welfare to Work strategy, the challenge becomes helping people to recognise and respond to this fact. To this end, links are being made between housing and employment advice so that people can be helped to appreciate the financial benefits of work. Meanwhile, advice about finding work serves to help people enter the labour market and realise the associated benefits. The Minister for Housing has suggested that such support and assistance might be taken into local neighbourhoods by outreach services provided through the Working Neighbourhoods Fund and run in community centres or schools on social housing estates (Flint 2008a). Social landlords have been encouraged to become involved in the delivery of such initiatives through the Working Neighbourhoods Fund, which was launched in 2007 and provides resources to local authorities to tackle worklessness and low levels of skills and enterprise in their most deprived areas. The Fund champions a twin-track approach, whereby (therapeutic) initiatives to engage people who are out of work are delivered alongside communitarian inspired efforts to 'galvanise community action on worklessness' and:

> 'The new Working Neighbourhoods Fund... will stimulate councils working with communities to take a fresh look at the problems of worklessness, and find proactive and innovative solutions... It provides for tangible rewards for local communities where targets are achieved. All members of the community could benefit from the financial incentives that will be introduced. Getting people into work would become a shared concern with everyone having something to gain from rising employment in their area. This new injection of peer support and peer pressure will go hand in hand with innovative approaches to engage people who have been out of work for lengthy periods. It is a new approach, a bold approach, and a community-driven approach.' (CLG and DWP 2007, Foreword.)

Social landlords have also been encouraged to remove any deterrents to work inherent within current management practices. In particular, attention has focused on responding to the suggestion by Hills (2007) that the rationing system that prioritises access to social housing on the basis of need means that people who want to move for job-related reasons are, in practice, required to choose between staying put or moving into the private rented sector and giving up the advantage of sub-market rents. On this basis, the limited options for moving within the sector might be considered a disincentive to work. Responding to this point, the Housing Green Paper (CLG 2007) committed CLG to consult on a new reasonable preference category, so that existing tenants seeking to move for work-related reasons receive higher priority in the allocation process. CLG is also investing in 18 new sub-regional choice-based lettings schemes intended to offer people the chance to move more easily across local authority boundaries (Cooper 2007; see also Pawson, Chapter 6).

These therapeutic interventions focus on helping people to recognise the benefits of work, and supporting them to realise these benefits by seeking and securing employment. It is also possible to discern an emerging emphasis within housing policy on more disciplinary interventions which focus on responsibilities and obligations. Access and security in social housing has always been dependent on tenants conforming to, and abiding by, certain conditions. In recent years, new elements of conditionality have been introduced. A particular emphasis has been placed on the need for tenants to conform to certain standards of conduct, in a bid to tackle antisocial behaviour (Flint 2006). Tenants can be evicted if they, or a member of their household, are deemed to have behaved in an inappropriate or unacceptable manner, and a pilot programme is exploring the viability of withdrawing Housing Benefit in such cases. It now appears that people might also be deemed undeserving of social housing on the basis of their attitude towards, and approach to, finding work. Referring to the therapeutic interventions that the Government is putting in place to help people out of worklessness, the Minister for Housing has commented that:

> 'If we are giving tenants a stronger voice, greater support and a better service, then it's only right that we have higher expectations in return. Social housing should be based around the principle of something for something.' (Flint 2008a.)

The 'something' being referred to, it appears, is the commitment to actively seek work, which the minister suggested could be formalised in 'commitment contracts' that new tenants would have to sign and which might subsequently be extended to existing tenants (Wintour 2008). Whether policy will pursue this disciplinary line in relation to worklessness remains to be seen, but it is certainly consistent with the Government's emphasis on a citizenship of obligations and earned rights.

To summarise, then, policy-makers assume a link between social housing and worklessness that is rooted in the cultural dispositions toward work that have been allowed to prosper, largely unchecked, on social housing estates. In response, the challenge is to reconstitute these neighbourhoods in a bid to promote the cultural change that supports the emergence of a more positive disposition towards formal paid work among residents. The pursuit of mixed communities is promoted as one way of reconstituting these neighbourhoods. In addition, therapeutic interventions are being developed in a bid to help social tenants recognise and realise the benefits of work, while disciplinary mechanisms are proposed as a means of penalising recalcitrant tenants who do not seek formal paid employment. The following section draws on rich empirical data from a survey of social tenants and worklessness to reflect upon the validity of these assumptions and the viability of the proposed response.

Exploring the links between social housing and worklessness

Three fundamental assumptions underpin the Government's diagnosis and prescribed response to the relatively high levels of worklessness among social tenants. Firstly, living in the social rented sector is assumed to expose people to area effects, including cultures of worklessness, that serve to distance them from formal paid work. Secondly, it is assumed that many social tenants are unaware of the work-related benefits of living in social housing and are unclear about the fact that work pays. Thirdly, various barriers are believed to be preventing social tenants realising the benefits of work. These include uncertainty about how to access work, confusion about the financial implications of being in work, and difficulties in moving for work-related reasons.

A recent study commissioned by the DWP set out to explore the validity of these assumptions through in-depth qualitative interviews with social tenants (Fletcher et al 2008a, 2008b). In total, 107 social tenants were interviewed in concentrated and pepper-potted areas of social housing in four local authority districts in England (Derby, Islington, Peterborough and Sheffield). A small group of 30 private tenants were also interviewed, providing a point of contrast against which to compare the experiences of social tenants and allowing any tenure-specific effects to be revealed. The discussion below draws on findings from this research to consider the three fundamental assumptions underpinning the policy response to evidence of relatively high levels of worklessness among social tenants. What is revealed is a far more complex and variegated situation than that presumed by contemporary policy.

Area effects and cultures of worklessness

Evidence of a lower cultural commitment to work among groups experiencing relatively high levels of worklessness has proved elusive (Gallie 2004). So it was among the social tenants interviewed, with analysis uncovering no evidence of a culture of worklessness among respondents in any of the case study neighbourhoods. Rather than being a homogenous group with a shared value-system that was resistant to work, the social tenants in each neighbourhood were revealed to be a varied group with different experiences, perspectives and needs. All the neighbourhoods had been affected by economic restructuring and social change, but this had impacted on individual residents in different ways. So, while some tenants had never worked, there were others who had a long record of stable employment. For some people, this period of employment had recently ended and the future was uncertain, although they remained committed to finding a new job. Some other tenants, meanwhile, were caught in the revolving door of low-paid work and unemployment.

While there was no evidence of a cultural resistance to work among social tenants, there was evidence of social norms and routines that represented barriers to formal paid employment. Typically these norms and routines centred around caring responsibilities (for children, partners, relatives and friends). Attitudes toward work among these people were not governed by economic considerations but rather were structured through moral considerations about what was the right and responsible thing to do. For example, lone parents talked about their moral responsibility to be a good parent, which might be compromised by entering formal paid work. However, there were also examples of some more damaging routines, including criminal activity and drug use. Involvement in the informal economy was rarely seen as an alternative to formal paid work, rather as an opportunity to top-up income from formal work or benefits.

In addition to evidence of social norms and routines resistant to work, two other area effects were uncovered – reported problems with postcode discrimination by employers, and the narrow spatial horizons among some local residents which served to restrict travel to work areas. These area effects were more readily apparent in neighbourhoods exhibiting a number of particular characteristics, in addition to persistent worklessness and poverty, including relatively low levels of residential mobility, with the population largely reproducing itself from within, and a strong sense of local identity and strong social networks between residents. Area effects were less evident in neighbourhoods not exhibiting these characteristics, which included some concentrated areas of social housing, as well as pepper-potted areas of social housing.

Evidence of area effects might be interpreted as supportive of efforts to create more diverse estates. However, this would be a mistake. Firstly, social tenants in all case studies areas were found to be positively disposed toward formal paid work, there was no evidence of a culture of worklessness. Secondly, despite sharing many characteristics, multiple area effects were only apparent in one of the four concentrated areas of social housing studied. The other three concentrated areas of social housing were found to differ little, in terms of area effects, to the pepper-potted areas of social housing. Thirdly, even on the estate where area effects were apparent, they were of secondary importance when it came to understanding experiences of worklessness, which were rooted in personal disadvantages, informed by individual roles and responsibilities, and set within the context of the local job market. Added to this, there is the fact that social mix is difficult to promote and even harder to sustain. What is more, little or no substantive evidence has emerged, either from large-scale quantitative studies (Manley et al 2007) or more locally-focused studies (Allen et al 2005; Atkinson and Kintrea 2000; Jupp 1999), that 'rubbing shoulders' with difference impacts in any substantial way on the outlook, dispositions or wellbeing of people living in mixed communities (see also Kintrea, Chapter 5).

Recognising that work pays

Contrary to a popular perception that social housing is a tired brand, a relic of a bygone era of welfare provision increasingly out of time in a world of individual choice and privatised consumption, there was near universal agreement among the social tenants (and many of the private tenants) interviewed that the sector provides a superior residential offer than the private rented sector for people on low incomes. Social tenants often talked, at length, about the benefits of living in the sector, which ranged from security of tenure through to the right to buy. Conspicuous by its absence in these discussions, however, was any reference to the work-related benefits of residing in the sector. No respondents identified social housing as raising any unique or particular barriers to work, but nor did many identify any work-related benefits of living in the sector, even when pushed on the issue. This finding would appear to confirm the suspicion that social tenants do not recognise the work-related benefits of living in the sector. However, pursuing this issue further, during interview, a clear distinction emerged between two groups of respondents.

On the one hand, there was a large group of respondents who struggled to recognise any work-related benefits of living in social housing. These were typically people who were not named tenants and therefore not responsible for the rent, people who had lived for much or all of their life in social housing and therefore had little or no experience of other tenures, and people who were distant from the labour market and not contemplating entering work in the near future. On the other hand, and in sharp contrast, there was a group of respondents who were able to point to ways in which residing in the social rented sector served to make work a more viable and realistic consideration. These respondents were typically named tenants who were responsible for the rent and who were 'closer' to the labour market. Three particular work-related benefits were recognised by these tenants, the importance of which was often underscored by reference to the very different situation encountered in the private rented sector: security of tenure, sub-market rents, and the more sympathetic and supportive attitude and practices of social landlords (for example, in managing rent arrears).

The issue of security emerged as particularly important. The security and stability offered by the social rented sector, which was frequently contrasted with the perceived insecurity of the private rented sector, provided an anchor point in lives that had often been in a state of flux and were characterised by uncertainty and turbulence. Confident about their residential security, social tenants often talked about being able to turn their attention to addressing other challenges in their life. For people more distant from the labour market this included health problems, disabilities and caring responsibilities. For people closer to the labour market these challenges included securing and maintaining work. This finding suggests that any moves to undermine security of tenure in the social rented sector are likely to have an adverse impact on levels of worklessness, as well as undermining the wellbeing of some of the most vulnerable tenants.

Although the work-related benefits of residing in the social rented sector were found to bring some people closer to the labour market, they did not necessarily render work a viable option. Sub-market rents were reported to make work a more financially feasible proposition, but many tenants remained concerned about the affordability of work. The security of tenure in the sector and the flexible and sympathetic attitude of social landlords were reported to reduce fears about the financial problems and associated threat to residential security encountered when entering work. However, many tenants remained concerned about debt problems and the prospect of rent arrears when moving off benefits and into work. These concerns are indicative of the breadth and depth of concerns that social tenants expressed about the financial viability and risks associated with taking up low-paid, insecure employment.

Contrary to the assertion that all work pays (Freud 2007), the social tenants interviewed had often concluded that work was 'unaffordable'. This conclusion was not always based on a full understanding of the financial consequences of entering work, with people often struggling to get to grips with the complex interaction between earnings, tax credits and Housing Benefit (see also Kemp, Chapter 4). For many people it was more a reflection of the financial uncertainties of work, in stark contrast to the certainty of their current situation. Concerns about the affordability of work were also inflected with assumptions about the problems that can be encountered returning to benefits in the event of being made unemployed. Underpinning all of these observations, however, was a keen understanding about the kinds of work available to people with low levels of human capital – low-paid, insecure or casual jobs – a reality of the contemporary labour market that makes no appearance in policy discussion of social housing and worklessness.

These findings suggest that helping people to recognise that work pays is likely to be a far greater challenge than policy recognises. For some people it is not clear that work does pay – indeed, some respondents talked about Jobcentre Plus 'better-off' calculations concluding that, financially speaking, it was not worth their while working. Even in situations where work does pay, the complexities of the tax and benefit system make this fact difficult to establish. Added to this confusion are concerns about the security of available work and the unpredictability of income, raising worries about budgeting when in work and managing the return to benefits as and when a short-term contract expires or a person is made redundant. Then there is the fact that people's actions are not solely governed by economic considerations, but are also informed by moral considerations (for example, being a good parent). People are therefore not always responsive to economic incentives or messages about financial gain. There are some obvious ways in which policy might respond to these factors, for example, moving to a single working-age benefit and placing greater emphasis on improving the human capital of social tenants to help improve their job prospects. Ultimately, however, such efforts run up against the reality of the contemporary labour market, and the low-paid and insecure nature of the jobs available to many of the people who are living in social housing.

Pointing out these realities is not to question whether social tenants would benefit from enhanced support, advice and assistance aimed at promoting greater labour market participation, or whether social landlords have a role to play in the provision of such support. There is no doubt that social landlords can play an important role here. The millions of pounds being spent on new housing and renewal programmes can support the generation of local jobs, increase the skills of local people, and promote local businesses (Mullins et al 2004). Social landlords are also well placed to provide support to help tenants secure and sustain employment by extending existing tenancy support activities. This might include work-related advice for workless social tenants, as well as housing-related support for working tenants, in a bid to limit concerns about difficulties paying the rent when in work, for example. However, two key questions need to be answered. Firstly, why should social landlords bother, there being no obvious housing management gain associated, in particular, with the extension of the housing management function into the provision of help to tenants to find work? Secondly, what role will social landlords play and how will their contribution be integrated into existing provision of employment advice and assistance? Expectations about what might be achieved by such supply-side interventions also need to be tempered, given that they do little to address the lack of stability and security in the low-paid segments of the contemporary labour market that serve to undermine the viability and attractiveness of work for social tenants close to the labour market.

Barriers to social tenants realising the benefits of work

No evidence emerged to suggest that social housing was a deterrent to work, or that the management of the sector presented any particular barriers to work. Contrary to the assumptions underpinning recent proposals contained in the Housing Green Paper (CLG 2007), none of the social tenants interviewed reported that problems moving within the social rented sector impacted on their chances of finding work, and respondents rarely indicated that relocating to another neighbourhood would improve their chances of finding work. Indeed, very few social or private tenants were willing to contemplate moving to improve their job opportunities, and only a small number reported they would move for a definite offer of work. This reluctance to move for work-related reasons is not surprising, given that job-related moves are typically made from a position of economic strength, and was explained by respondents with reference to the costs assumed to be associated with moving areas (severing of social ties and loss of key resources), which far outweighed the work-related benefits (the possibility of low-paid, insecure work). This is not to suggest that tenants were not keen to move. Many wanted to relocate, but the common drivers were the desire to move to a better neighbourhood or to move into more suitable accommodation.

These findings suggest that interventions intended to promote greater mobility within the sector are unlikely to have much impact on levels of worklessness. There are also a number of practical challenges associated with implementing the proposals contained in the Green Paper. For example, how is a sector already struggling to meet its statutory obligations to people in housing need going to meet responsibilities to an additional needs group (people seeking to move for work-related reasons), even if the numbers involved are likely to be relatively small? Why would social landlords want to support moves to increase mobility within the sector, given the practical headaches and associated costs of managing population churn? This is not to suggest that there are no tenants who would benefit from such interventions. Clearly, people living in locations isolated from employment opportunities and more qualified tenants seeking jobs not available in the local vicinity could benefit from such an initiative. The point is that the gains are likely to be limited.

The other important fact to be borne in mind by policy, as it pushes ahead with efforts to help tenants realise the benefits of work, is that many social tenants are too distant from the labour market for messages about why work pays, or advice about available job opportunities, to have any impact on their ability to consider looking for or finding work. Multiple and often severe problems were experienced by many of the social tenants interviewed, some of which were hidden or denied. These included mental and physical health problems; childcare responsibilities; debt, drug and alcohol dependence; and criminal records. Many tenants reported that they faced more than one of these barriers, as well as lacking skills, qualifications and work experience. These barriers also appeared to have a compound effect, each disadvantage adding extra burdens and bringing a corresponding reduction in a person's competitive position in the labour market. In sum, these problems are indicative of complex personal situations likely to inhibit labour market engagement. A final point to note is that they also represent experiences that are unlikely to be fully appreciated by traditional survey measures. This is an important factor that helps account for why previous analysis has struggled to explain the relatively high levels of worklessness within the social rented sector, allowing an unwarranted belief that being a social tenant is an independent predictor of worklessness to flourish.

Conclusion

There is no evidence that social housing represents a deterrent to work. Social tenants appear to have a positive disposition to work, and there is no evidence of cultures of worklessness on social housing estates. Nor does the management of social housing seem to be impacting on levels of worklessness within the sector. Rather, relatively high levels of worklessness in the social rented sector appear to reflect the personal disadvantages that distance many tenants from the labour market. These disadvantages are often severe and multiple in nature, yet frequently hidden and denied, a fact that helps explain why statistical analysis has struggled to explain relatively high levels of worklessness within the sector. People closer to the labour market often recognise the work-related benefits of living in the sector, but these benefits tend to be overshadowed by barriers to employment, including concerns about the affordability of work, which reflect the low-paid and insecure nature of employment available to many social tenants.

Supply-side orthodoxy and a fixation with cultural explanations have led policy to pathologise social housing and its tenants as the origin and cause of high levels of worklessness within the sector. However, there is no evidence to suggest that social housing is an independent predictor of worklessness, and policy prescriptions responding to this diagnosis are unlikely to cure the problem of worklessness in the social rented sector. Some recent developments, including improved support for social tenants moving into work, are to be welcomed, but the legacy of this policy agenda threatens to be more than benign failure. Distracting attention from addressing housing need in favour of a focus on efforts to govern the behaviour of social tenants in a bid to tackle various social ills, including worklessness, risks undermining the significant social gains that are being delivered by the sector. Moves to reduce security of tenure, for example, are unlikely to have any positive impact on levels of worklessness and will put at risk the wellbeing of some of the most vulnerable tenants. Such concerns could prove to be the tip of the iceberg however, as policy proceeds down a path that leads inexorably toward the logics of the Poor Law and the reprising of divisive distinctions between deserving and undeserving poor.

David Robinson is Professor of Housing and Public Policy and Deputy Director of the Centre for Regional Economic and Social Research, Sheffield Hallam University.

References

Allen, C., Camina, M., Casey, R., Coward, S. and Wood M., 2005. *Mixed tenure, twenty years on. Nothing out of the ordinary.* Coventry: CIH.

Atkinson, R. and Kintrea, K., 2000. Owner occupation, social mix and neighbourhood impacts. *Policy and Politics,* 28(1), p.93–108.

Cannizzaro, A. and Percival, N., 2006. *The impact of housing tenure on employment rates.* London: DWP.

CLG, 2007. *Homes for the future: more affordable, more sustainable.* (The Housing Green Paper) (Cmnd.7191) London: CLG.

CLG and DWP, 2007. *The working neighbourhoods fund.* London: CLG and DWP.

Cooper, Y., 2007. Social housing and investment. Statement by the Minister for Housing, 12 Dec.

Dorling, D., Rigby J., Wheeler, B., Ballas, D., Thomas, B., Fahmy, E., Gordon, D. and Lupton R., 2007. *Poverty, wealth and place in Britain, 1968 to 2005.* Bristol: Policy Press.

Fletcher, D., Gore, T., Reeve, K. and Robinson, D., 2008a. *Social housing and worklessness: key policy messages.* London: DWP.

Fletcher, D., Gore, T., Reeve, K. and Robinson, D., 2008b. *Social housing and worklessness: qualitative research findings.* London: DWP.

Flint, C., 2008a. Minister for Housing, Fabian Society Address, 5 Feb.

Flint, C., 2008b. Flint announces next steps to link housing advice and opportunities. CLG: London. 20 Mar.

Flint, J., ed., 2006. *Housing, urban governance and anti-social behaviour: perspectives, policy and practice.* Bristol: Policy Press.

Freud, D., 2007. *Reducing dependency, increasing opportunity: options for the future of welfare to work – an independent report to the Department for Work and Pensions.* London: DWP.

Gallie, D., 2004. *Resisting marginalisation: unemployment experience and social policy in the European Union.* Oxford: OUP.

Hills, J., 2007. *Ends and means: the future roles of social housing in England.* CASE Report 34, London: CASE and LSE. Available at: http://tinyurl.com/24ms5b

HM Treasury and DWP, 2003. *Full employment in every region.* London: TSO.

Manley, D., Doherty, J., Graham, E. and Boyle, P., 2007. *Social well-being for mixed tenure areas in Britain: 1991 to 2001.* European Network of Housing Research, Rotterdam. Available at: http://tinyurl.com/5g8pbp

Mullins, D., Beider, H. and Rowlands, R., 2004. *Empowering communities, improving housing: involving black and minority ethnic tenants and communities.* London: CLG.

Jupp, B., 1999. *Living together: community life on mixed tenure estates.* London: Demos.

SEU, 2004. *Jobs and enterprise in deprived areas.* London: ODPM.

Wintour, P., 2008. Labour: if you want a council house, find a job. The Guardian, 5 Feb, p.1.

Chapter 8

Need and demand, supply and quality

Glen Bramley

Introduction

This chapter considers the need and demand for affordable and social housing in England in the twenty-first century, looking both backwards at recent changes and forward into the immediate future. Recent changes in demand reflect problems of affordability in the mainstream market, as well as demographics, but within the social sector demand varies greatly depending on location and quality. We therefore also review the major drive to improve quality centring on the Decent Homes Standard, while also reflecting on the critical importance of neighbourhood quality and the functioning of local communities.

Housing need and demand

The current crisis of affordability has led to a recognition of the inadequacy of housing supply in general (Barker 2004), as well as in relation to social and affordable housing. Affordability is an increasingly important driver of demand for renting in general and social renting specifically, because of the dominant position in the housing system of owner occupation and the widespread aspiration towards home ownership. As house prices rise, relative to incomes, new households are less able to afford to buy and are forced to rent, perhaps indefinitely; increased competition for private rented housing may put more pressure on lower-income households to seek housing in the social sector, while existing social tenants are less able to afford to move out into home ownership or even to exercise the right to buy, and re-let availability declines. This is basically the story of the early twenty-first century, as house prices rose to unprecedented levels at the end of a long period of upswing, before this year's downturn consequent on the 'credit crunch'.

A statistical model designed by the present author shows how changes in affordability may be expected to impact on the need for additional affordable housing in different areas of the country. It takes account of demographics (new household formation, migration, and changes in the mix of household types); the existing backlog of unmet need (based on waiting lists and survey evidence on problems such as overcrowding); and the supply of re-lets from the existing social housing stock. This model indicates (see Figure 1, below) that in 2006 there was a very high level of need for additional affordable stock, totalling over 150,000 units per year. This figure is far in excess of recent levels of new social housing provision, currently around 25,000, although the Government plans to raise this to around 50,000. Figure 2, below, shows that new social rented provision averaged 40,000 per year in the early 1990s but fell to only 18,000 in the immediate years at the turn of the century, before rising again recently. In addition, provision of intermediate sector housing, such as shared ownership (Homebuy), would contribute to meeting some of this need, and Figure 2 shows the trend, indicating a fall up to the early part of the twenty-first century and then a recent rise. Low-cost home ownership currently accounts for over 40 per cent of 'affordable' provision.

Figure 1: Housing need numbers for 2006 by region

Region	Household growth	Net need (positives)	Surplus lettings	Net re-lets	Backlog need
North	8,400	886	4,919	23,463	58,169
Yorks & Humber	24,600	15,452	702	27,539	150,974
North West	27,400	8,346	6,009	47,222	132,612
East Midlands	21,000	8,252	1,676	23,151	81,632
West Midlands	19,800	5,070	3,522	34,184	77,244
South West	26,800	21,894	0	16,671	92,244
East	26,400	15,243	274	24,513	82,621
South East	32,800	31,043	196	27,039	119,377
London	39,200	48,524	387	26,692	202,050
England	226,400	154,710	17,685	250,473	996,924

Source: Bramley affordability model, baseline estimates for West of England Strategic Housing Market Assessment 2008.[1]

Figure 2: New social and affordable housing provision (average annual number)

Tenure	1991–1996	1996–2001	2001–2006	2006/07
Social rent	39,300	24,100	17,700	23,700
Low-cost home ownership	12,600	8,500	8,100	18,300
Total	51,900	32,200	25,800	42,000

Source: Wilcox 2007. Table 100, based on Housing Corporation Approved Development Programme.

[1] Note: All figures except backlog are annual flows, calculated at a local authority level. Household growth based on 2004-based household projections. Net need includes allowances for unaffordable new households, ten per cent of backlog, net migration and older households needing social housing, minus re-lets.

Contrasting Figures 1 and 2, it appears that there is a massive gap between need and supply, amounting to more than 100,000 units per year. The needs model assumes that a desirable target would be to meet newly arising need and also contribute to reducing the backlog of existing need by ten per cent each year. Clearly, in the conditions of 2006, provision of 42,000 would not be enough to reduce the backlog at all, with net need amounting to approximately 48,000 in London alone. Roughly 100,000 of the national need figure relates to the backlog and approximately 50,000 to newly arising need. We would therefore expect the backlog to continue to rise, as it has done over the last few years. Our own estimates suggest that the backlog rose by one-third between 2002 and 2006 (from 730,000 to almost one million).

In 2006, there were approximately 250,000 re-lets available, but this number had fallen from approximately 290,000 in 2002, primarily as a consequence of the tightening housing market. Worsening affordability increases demand from new households, while reducing the supply available. This change was particularly marked in the northern regions.

Figure 1 shows a figure for surplus lettings totalling about 18,000 in 2006. These surpluses arise in local authorities where the supply of re-lets exceeds new need plus the ten per cent backlog allowance. The localities affected are mainly in the northern regions. This surplus figure has fallen dramatically since 2002, when it stood at 76,000. Surplus measured in this way was a strong predictor of problems of low demand for social rented housing in many areas, particularly urban areas in the North and Midlands, in the late 1990s (Bramley 1998; Bramley et al 2000). This dramatic change suggests that the phenomenon of low demand has been very much reduced over the last few years, and is consistent with reports from practitioners in many of the affected areas.

Figure 3, overleaf, presents a forward projection of need, based on the affordability forecast discussed above. The regions are divided into three broad groupings for this purpose. Need rose sharply between 2002 and 2006. However, the rise was relatively modest in London, while being large in absolute magnitude in the South and particularly large in proportionate terms in the North and Midlands. Need is expected to fall again by 2011, but not to the levels of 2002. After that, it is expected to rise again, and in two of the three groupings this rise may be to a higher level than seen in 2006. One of the factors underlying this further rise in net need is the expected further decline in re-lets, partly reflecting the declining size of the social housing stock. The biggest increases in need, compared with 2002, are projected for the Yorkshire and Humber, the North West and the South West. Even with the government's proposed programme of 50,000 new social housing units per year, there will be little progress in reducing the backlog.

Figure 4, overleaf, provides the associated projection of surpluses. These will rise again to about 33,000 by 2011, then fall back to around the 20,000 level by 2016. This suggests that the issue of low demand, or excess supply of social renting, will persist in at least some areas.

Figure 3: Projected housing need by broad region 2002–2021

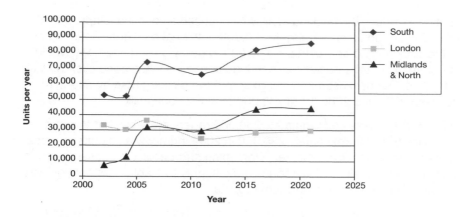

Source: Bramley affordability model, baseline projection for West of England Strategic Housing Market Assessment, 2008.

Figure 4: Surplus social lettings by broad region 2002–2021

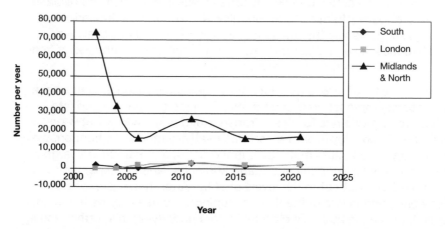

Source: Bramley affordability model, baseline projection for West of England Strategic Housing Market Assessment 2008.

Uneven demand at neighbourhood level

The analysis presented so far emphasises the extent to which need and demand for social/affordable housing varies between regions. However, the unevenness of demand is also an important feature at a finer geographical scale.

Figure 5, overleaf, summarises the picture using six deprivation bandings and four broad regions. Net needs are expressed as a percentage of resident households, with bars above the zero-line indicating shortages and bars below the line indicating surpluses.

In the North and Midlands, the most deprived 20 per cent of wards have substantial surpluses, while in the South the most deprived 10 per cent of wards also show surpluses. Only in London, are all categories of ward in shortage. In the North and Midlands, shortages are only apparent in the most affluent 40 per cent of wards – typically more rural or suburban areas. In the South, shortages are apparent in the more affluent 60 per cent of wards, as well as overall.

It is, in a sense, artificial to look at needs at this neighbourhood level, because wards are part of wider housing market areas within which people seek housing opportunities. Nevertheless, these figures do indicate features of the housing system, and the role of social housing within it, which are quite meaningful. Deprived wards tend to be wards with a lot of social housing and many re-lets; they contribute more to supply than to demand. More affluent wards have less available social housing and lower turnover rates, while they generate more potential demand because they are less affordable. Lower-income households who cannot enter the market in these more favoured areas will tend to have to move to the more deprived areas, where housing is more affordable and where there is more social housing available. These areas tend to be unpopular, and are less likely to be areas of choice. We go on later to present other evidence on the unhappiness of many residents with conditions in these areas. Some of these adverse conditions, such as higher crime rates, antisocial behaviour, poorer schools, and worse environments, tend to be exacerbated by the concentration of poorer and more vulnerable people in these areas. But the housing system tends to reinforce the process whereby these groups become concentrated there (see Kintrea, Chapter 5).

While there is a natural tendency for the housing market to reproduce these patterns of concentration of lower-income groups in certain areas, it is a matter of policy whether new investment in social housing serves to reinforce or counter this tendency. The evidence from data on recent patterns of new housing association lettings indicates that recent investment patterns have tended to reinforce this pattern. This is shown in Figure 6, overleaf, which confirms that new housing association building was concentrated in the most deprived wards in the three time periods considered up to 2005/06. New social housing has frequently been associated with regeneration schemes that have targeted deprived neighbourhoods (which were often also low-demand areas), and has also tended to be located on land already held for social housing purposes on existing estates. However, this is not the pattern which would have been indicated if more attention had been paid to the kind of evidence of need and demand represented by Figure 5, overleaf.

The issue of social mix and balance in neighbourhoods has risen up the policy agenda for planning and regeneration, and this evidence suggests that the contribution of new social housing has not been as helpful as it might have been in this respect (see also Chapter 5). Paradoxically, Figure 6, below, suggests that new private housing made a much bigger contribution to promoting social mix during this period than new social housing did, and this contribution increased over time. However, in the future, with a larger social housing programme, and the more systematic exploitation of section 106 planning agreements to ensure the inclusion of social housing within general private housing developments, the tendency for social housing development to be concentrated in deprived areas may begin to change.

Figure 5: Net need for affordable housing by deprivation level and broad region, 2006 (based on ward level analysis).

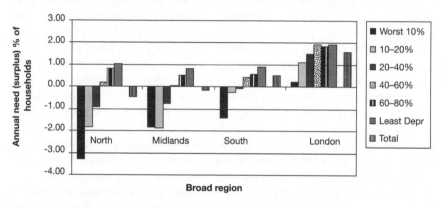

Source: Bramley and Watkins (2008 forthcoming) Market Assessment, 2008.

Figure 6: New build by sector, ward deprivation and time period.

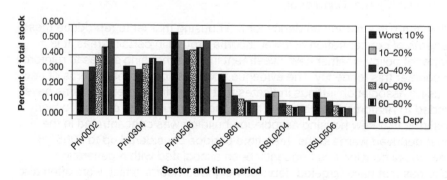

Source: Bramley et al, 2007, Figure 11.

Low demand revisited

We have already touched on low demand when referring to localities with surpluses of social lettings, relative to a standard measure of demand. This suggested that the phenomenon had reduced in scale, but had not been completely eliminated and may tend to recur in some areas. Low demand will reflect the wider housing market conditions of an area, but it tends to manifest itself in particular neighbourhoods. Typically, these are relatively deprived areas, often dominated by social housing but also often areas of older, poorer quality housing in a mixture of tenures (Bramley et al 2000). Symptoms include higher vacancy rates, higher turnover, low prices, and difficulties selling homes. Since 2003, many of the worst affected areas have been incorporated in a special programme of housing market renewal managed by pathfinder organisations on a partnership basis. These programmes typically comprise a mixture of demolition, improvement, new build and tenure diversification.

It is interesting to try to gauge, from a range of relevant indicators, how far the problems of low demand in these areas have been alleviated, in the recent period of high housing market pressure and selective intervention. Figure 7, below, presents a composite measure based on five key indicators for three time periods (2001, 2003/04, and 2005/06). It compares three deprivation bandings for the northern and midland regions. Values of the index significantly above 100 indicate low demand problems. It can be seen that there was quite a sharp fall in the incidence of low demand in the more deprived wards between 2001 and 2003/04. However, in the next two years the index values worsened slightly in the most deprived 20 per cent of wards, particularly in the North.

Figure 7: Composite low-demand indices 2000–2006

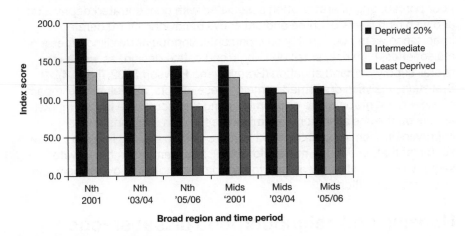

Source: Bramley et al, 2007, Figure 19.

Low-demand incidence reduced markedly in all pathfinder areas between 2001 and 2003/04. However, in the most recent period covered, between 2003/04 and 2005/06, low-demand incidence was relatively static for these areas overall. In a couple of cases (Manchester-Salford and Liverpool-Merseyside) low-demand incidence appears to have increased. Vacancy rates were a specific indicator which deteriorated during this period in some of these areas. Demolitions were also significant in a number of cases. Demolitions could have the effect of eliminating vacancies which would otherwise have risen further, but the process of preparing areas for demolition could, in the short term, serve to increase vacancies. This may therefore be a transitional effect as the pathfinder programmes geared up.

The low-demand indicators just discussed are a composite of measures relating to both the private market and the social sector. In assessing prospects for the social sector it is useful to focus in particular on areas with a lot of social housing. The *Transforming places* database shows a fairly clear picture, which is quite encouraging in relation to recent trends at any rate. (Bramley et al 2007.) At the beginning of the decade, low demand was quite prevalent in wards with more social housing, particularly in the northern and midland regions, but not in London. Between 2001 and 2005, low-demand incidence fell in all areas, but it fell more significantly in the areas with more social renting than in those with less social renting, and this systematic pattern applied in all regions. Therefore, we can say that the tendency for low demand to be associated with areas of predominantly social housing weakened during this period.

The studies of low demand carried out between 1998 and 2000 identified a range of causal factors, using a mixture of sources of evidence, including practitioner views and statistical modelling. Practitioner views about the causal factors behind social sector low demand emphasised stigma and poor perceptions of areas, often associated with concentrated deprivation and with high levels of crime and antisocial behaviour. Of moderate importance were poor quality environments, unpopular dwelling types (eg, maisonettes, high rise, small dwellings) and estate design, as well as the overall supply/demand situation (Bramley and Pawson 2002, Table 4). Statistical analyses confirmed some of these effects, as well as the impact of wider demographic and economic change, although the labour market effects on the social sector were mixed because in some instances improved economic conditions led to more people moving into the private sector (at that time much more affordable). Low demand in the private sector was more strongly related to economic conditions, oversupply and poor stock condition.

Housing and neighbourhood dissatisfaction

It is clear that social renters tend to exhibit more dissatisfaction with both their homes and their neighbourhoods, compared with people in other tenures, particularly owner occupation, when questioned in large-scale surveys such as the *Survey of English Housing.* Figure 8, below, looks at some key indicators of this kind, distinguishing local authority and housing association renters and, in the latter case, further distinguishing relatively newer stock from older housing. For three of the four indicators considered, the worst scores are for local authority renters, but the scores for housing associations are not much better and, disappointingly, renters in the newest housing association stock are, if anything, slightly less satisfied than those in older housing association stock.

Figure 8: Indicators of dissatisfaction and neighbourhood problems by tenure, and newness

Tenure	Dissatisfied with area (%)	Dissatisfied with home (%)	Neighbourhood problems score	Difficulty Access Services (%)	Sample
Own	7.2	2.8	0.44	16.4	23,415
Private rent	8.0	10.5	0.50	19.5	3,502
Local authority rent	15.4	15.9	0.84	27.9	3,537
Housing association pre-1985	12.7	13.8	0.78	27.5	1,838
Housing association 1986–1995	11.8	11.1	0.81	28.8	336
Housing association post-1996	13.4	13.3	0.82	23.5	231

Source: Survey of English Housing 2004/05–2005/06.

These descriptive data do present a sobering picture of the problems facing many social renters and social renting areas. However, they do not in themselves demonstrate what factors are causing these patterns. They may reflect social and demographic characteristics of the households themselves, or different features of the neighbourhoods where they live. We therefore applied statistical models to try to tease out the influence of different factors while controlling for other factors. This modelling exercise found that neighbourhood dissatisfaction was greater for households in terraced houses, flats and homes without gardens, and that this applied to all tenures, as well as to social renters. Dissatisfaction was greater in areas with more poverty, and for social renters it rose in areas with more social housing. For new housing association residents it was greater in higher density areas. In all cases, dissatisfaction was concentrated in areas with more new housing association development. This could be because of the disruptive effects of new development/redevelopment, or because new builds have been deliberately concentrated in the 'worst' areas, or because the residents of new housing association housing have greater vulnerability or social problems. The results for modelling home dissatisfaction are generally similar.

Decent homes

In the 1990s, a major challenge identified for housing policy was the large backlog of disrepair in the public sector stock at the same time as awareness was growing of the need to promote higher standards in relation to a wider range of issues, including energy efficiency given the problems of fuel poverty. This led to the adoption of a new set of standards known as the Decent Homes Standard and the ambitious target to bring the social sector estate up to a general standard of decency by 2010. A major programme of investment was instituted, using a variety of mechanisms including accelerated stock transfers, arms-length management organisations, use of the Private Finance Initiative and major repairs allowances within the Housing Revenue Account.

Figure 9: Non-decent homes by tenure 1996–2005

Tenure	1996	2001	2005
	%	%	%
Local authority	53.9	41.7	33.7
Housing association	47.6	33.1	23.8
All social sector	52.6	38.9	29.2
Owner-occupied	39.7	29.2	24.9
Private rented	62.4	50.7	40.7
All private sector	42.6	31.9	27.1

Source: Wilcox (2007) Table 23b, derived from English House Condition Surveys.

Progress towards achievement of this goal can be gauged from the data in Figure 9, above. In 1996, a slight majority of social housing fell below the Decent Homes Standard. By 2005, this had fallen to 29.2 per cent, a reduction of 45 per cent. The rate of reduction was greater in the housing association sector, probably due to the effects of stock transfer and the accelerated repairs and improvements associated with this mechanism. Nevertheless, the full achievement of the standard within the envisaged timescale remains challenging and somewhat uncertain. However, it is still true that the rate of improvement is greater in the social sector than in the private sector, so there is some prospect that in this respect the relative position, and potential attractiveness, of the social sector may be improved.

Decent physical standards may be a necessary condition for social housing to achieve a rehabilitation, in terms of its reputation and appeal to potential tenants, but on its own it may not be sufficient. The evidence presented above indicates that neighbourhood social conditions and associated environmental problems are strongly related to dissatisfaction. This suggests that measures to address these will be equally important. Such measures will include neighbourhood management activities to tackle crime, antisocial behaviour and environmental problems, but also allocation and structural redevelopment activities aimed at eliminating the concentration of poverty and associated social problems (see Kintrea, Chapter 5).

Strategy for supply of social housing

In light of the evidence presented in this chapter, what should the government's strategy for housing supply be, and what should the role of social housing be within this? The post-1980s policy environment has been one where market solutions have been prioritised by all parties, yet the market has failed to a significant degree in ensuring an adequate supply of housing or a smooth progression towards a situation where most households can gain access to affordable solutions. The Government has rediscovered the need to have a pro-active policy for supply (Bramley 2007), and has conspicuously failed to abolish the cycle of 'boom and bust' in the housing market.

There are a number of elements to the menu of policies which are required to overcome these problems, and we consider them in turn.

Social housing investment

Barker recommended higher investment in new social rented housing and the Government has also taken this on board, with plans to raise output to around 50,000 units per year in England, plus an additional 20,000 of intermediate sector housing. Additional public investment in grants to support this has been committed, although it is expected that some of this extra provision will be delivered without any grant and instead facilitated chiefly through the use of planning agreements (see below), but will also be assisted by innovations in delivery mechanisms combining private with public funding and more efficient procurement by housing associations. But as the Bramley model indicates, this modest increase in supply (even if achieved) will barely meet newly arising need, and will fail to make any inroads into the backlog in unmet housing needs that is likely to continue to rise. While pressures on social housing supply are greatest in London, projected increases in unmet need are proportionately largest in the North and Midlands. In all regions, it is important that efforts are made to avoid concentrating new social housing in the most deprived wards, in order to address both demand and social-mix objectives, albeit that the high land costs in non-deprived areas are undoubtedly a serious constraint (see also Kintrea, Chapter 5).

Section 106 planning agreements

An important innovation of the 1990s entails local planning authorities requiring most new developments to contain a mix of affordable and private housing, or to make equivalent financial contributions towards affordable provision elsewhere. The key mechanism is the planning agreement, under section 106 of the 1990 planning legislation, backed up by evidence of local needs. This policy was initially slow to deliver but by the beginning of the twenty-first century a majority of new affordable housing was being delivered in this way. The underlying logic is that development gains in land value should be used to subsidise affordable housing, but confusion about how this should or should not be combined with public grants has limited the extent to which, so far, this housing has been additional to that which would have happened anyway (Crook et al 2002; Monk et al 2005). However, more rigorous application of these policies has considerable potential, particularly in the higher-priced southern regions where need is greatest. This approach also helps to promote more mixed and balanced communities, as well as sourcing sites for housing associations to build on or acquire stock.

Intermediate sector provision

Affordable housing embraces both traditional social renting and intermediate tenures, such as shared ownership/equity (promoted now as 'Homebuy' in England) and intermediate rent-level accommodation. There is considerable logic in promoting such tenures, because they make smaller demands per unit on scarce subsidy resources, have the potential to be almost self-financing in the longer term and are capable of attracting private finance. In addition, these tenures also meet widespread aspirations for home ownership, greater choice (which may be important for client groups such as key workers), and promoting mixed-tenure and mixed-income communities. These tenures fit well with the section 106 mechanism and we have already seen that a growing share of affordable provision comes in this form. It also fits with the pattern of need, whereby in regions of poor affordability many working households cannot enter the market without some level of assistance. Nevertheless, there are continuing problems with the creation of effective vehicles, particularly using private finance in the current disrupted mortgage market conditions.

Right to buy?

What should the role of the right to buy be in this new environment? Traditionally, the social housing sector has been broadly hostile to the right to buy, because it is seen as eroding the social housing stock and giving financial benefits to better-off tenants at the expense of the poor. On the other hand, the policy has been popular with the public, has helped to meet aspirations for home ownership among lower-income groups, and in some circumstances has helped to create mixed and stable communities (Jones and Murie 2006). While in earlier periods the discounts to right to buy purchasers have been very generous, recent restrictions and the rising market have made even right to buy properties unaffordable for most tenants, and numbers of sales have fallen to low levels. Wilcox (2006) has argued that somewhat higher discounts would still represent value-for-money for the public purse. However, it has also been contended that the right to buy creates a disincentive for the provision of new social housing, and in Scotland this has led the SNP-led Government to suspend the Right to Buy scheme for new council housing and to question whether it should be extended to the housing association sector. There have also been concerns that, in lower-demand and more deprived neighbourhoods, right to buy dwellings tend to end up in the hands of irresponsible private landlords, which makes the task of neighbourhood management even more challenging.

Conclusion

Housing affordability has become a major issue in the UK, having deteriorated to an unprecedented degree in the twenty-first century, notwithstanding this year's fall in house prices (which has, in any case, failed to improve the accessibility of home ownership because of the contraction in mortgage availability). This has led to a demonstrable increase in the need and demand for affordable and social housing. So far, the supply of such housing falls far short of the levels of need that are indicated. The Government has acknowledged that housing supply is a major challenge and has adopted new policies to promote supply on a large scale. It has also set targets in relation to affordability as a key outcome, and has acknowledged and responded to the call for a substantial increase in the supply of new social housing, as well as a wider range of intermediate sector affordable provision.

Compared with the relatively low-key approach of the 1990s, this change is surely a very welcome one for the social housing sector. Housing has risen to near the top of the policy agenda and there is a real prospect of serious investment in new provision to expand the sector. Problems of low demand have been very much reduced, if not completely eliminated. There has also been a major and sustained drive to bring the existing social housing stock up to the Decent Homes Standard, which should be substantially achieved by the beginning of the next decade. Taken together with the emphasis on mixed and balanced communities, this might be expected to reinforce a situation where social housing becomes more a tenure of choice, with a broader range of households living within it.

However, this positive spin on the current conjuncture of events and policies needs to be tempered by consideration of a number of clouds on the horizon, not to mention some dark clouds which seem to be almost directly overhead. In the short term, the credit crunch threatens the smooth functioning of the housing market, worsens access to the market, and is already reducing new market supply. In the medium term, it is not clear that public finances are strong enough to support the range of investments in both social housing and in growth-supporting infrastructure, which are required to deliver the supply strategy. Rising costs, including those associated with low-energy homes, will also affect supply. Local authorities and regional planning bodies in the southern English regions are not wholly persuaded of the need to build vastly more housing, and these views may gain a stronger hearing under any future government of a different political hue.

Whether social housing will really become a tenure of choice for mainstream working households is also questionable. Although new developments may be attractively mixed, a large part of the existing stock will remain in its present configuration, with large concentrations of low-income, often workless, and/or vulnerable households, living in areas with significant social problems affecting quality of life, health and educational opportunities. Inequalities in income and wealth have continued to increase, so entrenching the differences between these communities and those that are more favoured (see Kintrea, Chapter 5). It is not clear that any changes in the terms and conditions of social sector tenancies, or in access and allocation arrangements, provide any 'magic bullets' to overcome these disparities. Reducing security of tenure would seem likely to make social housing even less attractive as a housing solution, removing one of its distinctive advantages over private renting or marginal home ownership. Removing the right to buy would also reduce a key intrinsic attraction of a social tenancy. Choice-based allocation (discussed by Pawson in Chapter 6) still has to contend with the wide differences in attractiveness of different parts of the sector and the inverse relationship between this and the availability of lettings.

Glen Bramley is Professor of Housing and Planning/Urban Studies at the School of the Built Environment, Heriot-Watt University, Edinburgh.

References

Barker, K., 2003. *Review of housing supply: securing our future housing needs – interim report, analysis.* London: TSO and HM Treasury.

Barker, K., 2004. *Review of housing supply, delivering stability: securing our future housing needs – final report and recommendations.* London: TSO and HM Treasury.

Bramley, G., 1998. Housing surpluses and housing need. In S. Lowe, S. Spencer and P. Keenan, eds. *Housing abandonment in Britain: studies in the causes and effects of low demand housing.* York: Centre for Housing Policy, University of York.

Bramley, G., 2007. The sudden rediscovery of housing supply as a key policy challenge. *Housing Studies,* 22(2), p.221–242.

Bramley, G., Pawson, H. and Third, H., 2000. *Low demand housing and unpopular neighbourhoods.* London: DETR.

Bramley, G., Fitzpatrick, S., Karley, N.K., Monk, S. and Pleace, N., 2005. *Evaluation of English housing policy since 1975 – theme 1, report: supply, need and access.* London: ODPM.

Bramley, G. and Karley, N.K., 2005. How much extra affordable housing is needed in England? *Housing Studies,* 20(5), p.685–715.

Bramley, G. and Leishman, C., 2005. Planning and housing supply in two-speed Britain: modelling local market outcomes. *Urban Studies,* 42(12), p.2213–2244.

Bramley, G., Leishman, C., Karley, N. K., Morgan, J. and Watkins, D., 2007. *Transforming places: housing investment and neighbourhood market change.* York: JRF.

Bramley, G. and Pawson, H., 2002. Low demand for housing: extent, causes and UK policy implications. *Urban Studies,* 39(3), p.393–422.

Bramley, G. and Watkins, C. Affordability and supply: the rural dimension. *Planning Practice and Research* (forthcoming).

Cambridge Centre for Housing and Planning Research, 2003. *2003 update of reports from Shelter's Housing Investment Project (SHIP).* Cambridge: CCHPR.

CLG, 2007. *Homes for the future: more affordable, more sustainable.* (The Housing Green Paper) (Cmnd.7191). London: CLG.

CLG, 2007. *Strategic housing market assessment guidance.* London: CLG.

CLG, 2006. *Planning policy statement 3: housing.* London: CLG.

Crook, T., Currie, J., Jackson, A., Monk, S., Rowley, S., Smith, K. and Whitehead, C., 2002. *Planning gain and affordable housing: making it count.* York: YPS.

Hills, J., 2007. *Ends and means: the future roles of social housing in England.* CASE Report 34. London: CASE and LSE. Available at: http://tinyurl.com/24ms5b

Jones, C. and Murie, A., 2006. *The right to buy: analysis and evaluation of a housing policy.* Oxford: Blackwell.

Monk, S., Crook, T., Lister, D., Rowley, S., Short, C. and Whitehead, C., 2005. *Land and finance for affordable housing: the complementary roles of social housing grant and the provision of affordable housing through the planning system.* York: JRF.

National Housing and Planning Advice Unit, 2007. *Developing a supply range for the supply of new homes across England – a discussion paper.* Tichfield: NHPAU.

NHPAU, 2008. *Meeting the housing requirements of an aspiring, growing and prosperous nation – advice to the Housing Minister about the housing supply range to be tested by the regional planning authorities.* Tichfield: NHPAU.

Wilcox, S., 2005. *Affordability and the intermediate market.* York: JRF.

Wilcox, S., 2006. A financial evaluation of right to buy. *UK Housing Review,* 15th edn, p.11–20. Coventry: CIH.

Wilcox, S., 2007. *The affordability of private housing in Great Britain: local measures of the affordability of owner occupied and private rented housing.* London: Hometrack.

Chapter 9

Understanding the demand for social housing

Sarah Monk, Anna Clarke and Christine Whitehead

Introduction

The Government needs to understand more about the demand (and need) for social rented housing for a number of reasons. One is simply to be better able to meet future demand in terms of ensuring that social housing is built in the right locations, and the right mix of house types (flats, houses) and sizes (number of bedrooms) is provided. Similarly, affordable housing needs to be provided in the appropriate tenure – subsidised rented or low-cost home ownership – and with a level of affordability.

The Government also needs to understand where social housing is not in demand. Low demand for specific locations, types or sizes of dwelling results in empty units, making a block or street unattractive and thus adding to the difficulty of letting other properties. This can escalate so that a whole area becomes low demand. There are then financial implications for social landlords because rental income is reduced by high rates of vacancy, and local businesses and services can be adversely affected because there is a smaller population to serve. It is also important not to continue building additional affordable homes in such areas (apart from replacement) and there may be a case for quite drastic stock rationalisation where there is low demand for certain types of property.

Secondary data can tell us a good deal about demand for social housing, and detailed questionnaires, along with interviews and focus groups, can add the more qualitative information that cannot be covered by the standard sources such as household surveys. This chapter is based on both primary and secondary data analysis conducted for a major study commissioned by the Housing Corporation in 2007–08.[1]

---

[1] The research comprised a range of different methods:
* review of existing literature and other studies
* secondary data analysis
* omnibus survey of current social tenants and private sector tenants with low incomes
* exit survey of those leaving social housing, including telephone interviews
* focus group discussions with BME households and other particular groups.
Summary findings and a source document are available at http://tinyurl.com/6fafok

The study focused on the drivers of demand – demographic, spatial and economic – and this chapter is organised according to these drivers, drawing some overall conclusions and finishing by looking at what is likely to happen in the future. The chapter also considers the process of 'residualisation' of social housing, the main groups in social housing, and what sort of housing social tenants want.

The main message is that there is no shortage of demand for social rented housing, and there are many households who prefer it to other options, but overall this is a changing group and this has implications for how social housing is provided.

Demographic impacts on demand

A number of interesting findings emerged from the analysis of the impacts of demography on demand (see Figures 1–4, below) using the *Survey of English Housing* and the Census. Those in younger age groups, rather than middle or older, were more likely to apply for social housing in the first place, although this was related to need rather than aspirations. Black and minority ethnic (BME) households were more likely to actively want to live in the sector, but there is variation between groups in terms of how likely they are to actually live in the sector. Households with children were more likely than those without children to prefer social housing to renting in the private sector. There was also some demand from owner-occupiers who could no longer afford their home. These were mainly separating couples but there were also people relocating and people whose income had fallen since they started to purchase.

Figure 1: Previous tenure of entrants to social housing

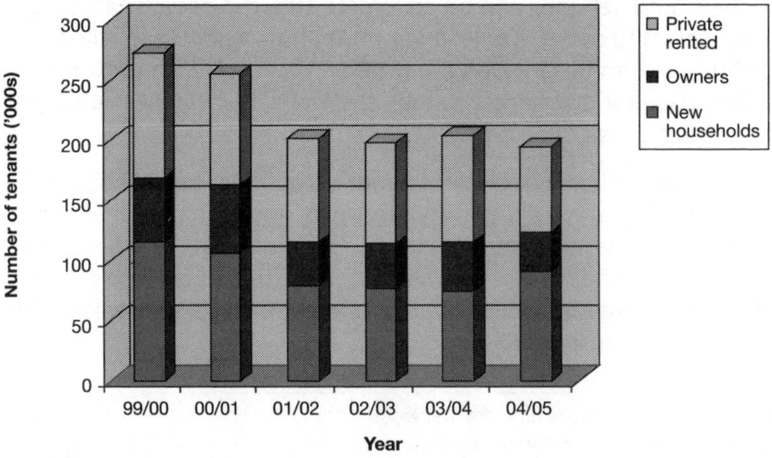

Source: Survey of English Housing 2005/06.

The profile of the social sector depends partly on who applies, but also on allocation policies that give priority to those in greatest housing need. This means, in practice, that households who are in unsuitable housing have priority. New entrants to social housing are mainly under 45, couples and singles with children, and single persons from all age groups. There are also elderly homeowners with increasing health needs.

Overall, the sector houses more people at the two ends of the age range, with fewer people aged 45 to 74. There are proportionately more single people and single parents than in the population as a whole, and more people with special needs.

Figure 2: Age of social tenants by household type

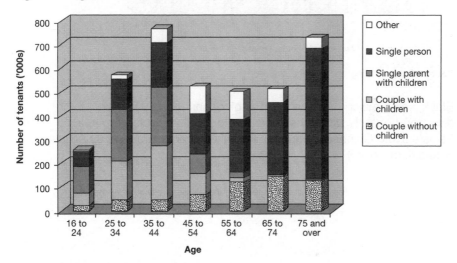

Source: Survey of English Housing 2005/06.

Households with a member who has a disability are more likely to be in social housing (see Figure 3, overleaf). Numerically, most of these are in the older age groups, although the proportion with a disability living in social housing is much higher relative to other tenures in the under 65 age groups. This suggests that developing an illness or handicap while still of working age is more likely to mean people live in social housing.

Figure 3: Households with a disability

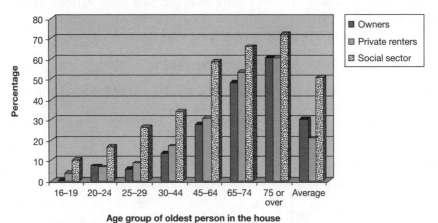

Source: Survey of English housing, 2005/06

Black, some mixed heritage and Bangladeshi households live disproportionately within the social sector, while people from Indian, Pakistani and Chinese groups are less likely than average to do so (see Figure 4, opposite).

Figure 4: Ethnic groups in social housing

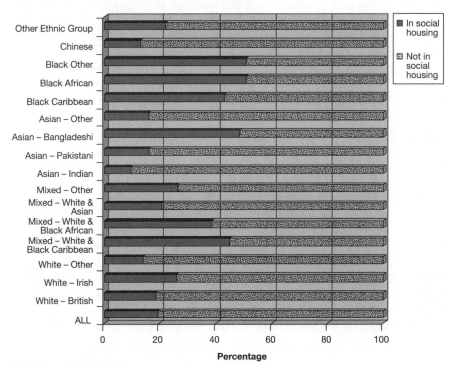

Source: Census, 2001.

There are considerable variations between ethnic groups in terms of the household types within social housing. Black households entering social housing are overwhelmingly single people or lone parents. Very few Black Caribbean couple households enter, even with children. Black households very often enter when young as a route into independent living (the Continuous Recording System (CORE) 2006).

Single people make up the great majority of white Irish households entering social housing. Households from other white backgrounds are more likely to be single parents or couples with children.

Pakistani and Bangladeshi households are more likely to be couples with children, and very often enter as a result of overcrowding. There are many more 'other household types with children' among these groups – often multi-generational households. Indian households entering the tenure are mostly single people, although there are also some couples with children, single parents escaping overcrowding, and some other household types with children.

Most minority ethnic groups entering housing association housing are spatially concentrated, mainly around the large cities. For example, 62 per cent of Bangladeshi households entering RSL housing did so in only ten local authorities.

There are also more large families in social housing than in the population as a whole, but the sector lacks the accommodation to ensure that they are well housed. This is one reason why overcrowding is relatively high compared to other tenures, although, as is demonstrated in Chapter 1, in terms of rooms per person the UK performs very well internationally across all income groups. Overcrowding is a particular problem in large cities, such as London, where small flats are the most common type of available supply, because those families lucky enough to obtain larger units tend to stay put, understandably.

'Residualisation' of social housing

During the 1980s, there was what has been termed a residualisation of social housing as working households increasingly left the sector, often through the Right to Buy scheme. In the 1990s, the changes were less pronounced, although there continued to be an increase in the proportion of 'other economically inactive' households which includes lone parents, sick and disabled households, students and carers. At the same time, the age distribution of social tenants became focused on those at either end of the age range, as older households were unable to take advantage of the right to buy and over time were replaced by younger households who were too poor to make use of it, or not (yet) able to access it. Figure 5, below, shows changes in the sector over the last few years in absolute terms.

Figure 5: Economic activity of social tenants 1999–2006

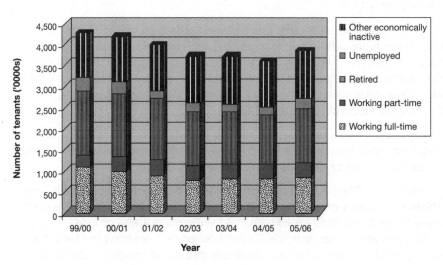

Source: Survey of English Housing 2005/06.

It is well known that the social sector has long been declining in size. However, although it continues to decline as a proportion of all housing, it increased in absolute size in 2005/06 for the first time in many years, and this is reflected in Figure 5, opposite. This was the result of changing regulations regarding the Right to Buy scheme, which has therefore fallen significantly, coupled with increasing rates of new build.

The main component of change to the sector as a whole over the last five years has come about largely from a decline in the number of retired households within the sector, most of whom presumably died rather than moved into other tenures.

In terms of the demographic drivers of demand for social housing in the future, there are predicted to be the following changes in the composition of the sector:

- smaller proportions of all households living in the sector
- increasing proportions of one-person households, reflecting the national pattern
- increasing proportions of lone parents, which also reflects the national picture
- increasing proportions of BME households, again reflecting the national picture
- a small increase in the very old age groups (80+), also reflecting national trends, and
- a reduction in those aged over 60.

This last factor arises because the very large cohort aged 70–79 in 2001 will be gone by 2021 and younger age groups have had lower propensities to live in social housing or have left through the right to buy.

Spatial impacts on demand

There are considerable differences between regions in terms of both demand and supply of social housing. For historical reasons, social housing was built in greater amounts in some areas than others. In more recent years some areas have lost stock faster than others as a result of the Right to Buy scheme, and rates of more recent building have varied according to differing levels of land availability, funding and need for affordable housing. Figure 6, overleaf, shows the current pattern of supply.

Figure 6: Regional variations in supply of social housing

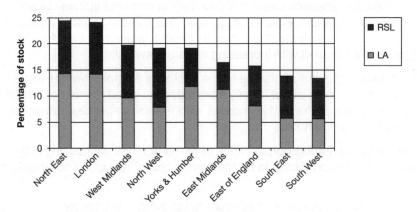

Source: Housing Strategy Statistical Appendix 2005/06.

Demand for social housing varies across the country (see Figure 7, below). Relative to supply of new social lettings, demand is highest in London, followed by Yorkshire & Humberside, and the South West.

Figure 7: Households on the housing register (April 2006) per social letting in the past 12 months

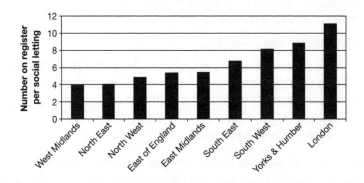

Source: Housing Strategy Statistical Appendix 2005/06.

There is low demand in parts of the North and the Midlands, but it has been falling quite fast and the differences between regions in terms of vacant dwellings are no longer significant (this may be due to demolitions, but also the overall rise in the cost of market housing) (see also Bramley, Chapter 8). The quality of the local neighbourhood is crucial to demand. There is a strong perception that social housing is located in bad areas and this reduces demand. One major reason given for moving both within the social housing sector and out of the sector, is to move to a good area. Fear of racism also affects the locational choices of many BME groups.

There are also spatial differences in the profile of social tenants. Yorkshire and the East Midlands have more older people, and London has the fewest (see Figure 8, below). There are more children in the social sector in London and the South East, yet the North has more larger dwellings. The proportion of tenants who are in employment is higher in the South and East (but not in London), especially among new entrants (see Figure 9, overleaf). For those in work, incomes are higher in London. London generally has a much more ethnically diverse population in the social sector, with over 40 per cent of tenants from a BME group – this compares with only 5 per cent in the North West and South West. This is not just associated with the social sector, but reflects the diversity of London's population as a whole. The same is true for the regions with few BME tenants – there are fewer in social housing but there are fewer in the region in the first place.

Figure 8: Regional differences in social tenants – age

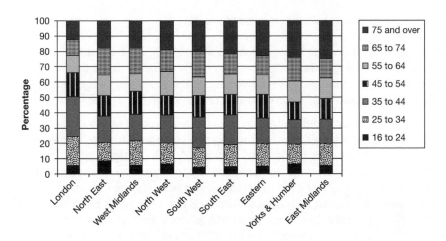

Source: Survey of English Housing 2005/06.

Figure 9: Regional differences in new entrants – age

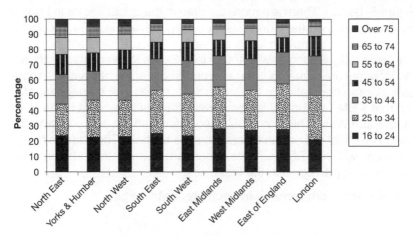

Source: The Continuous Recording System (CORE) 2006/07.

Figures 8 and 9 show that while there are strong regional differences in the age profile of existing tenants, the profile of new entrants to the sector shows much less variation. Even where supply is apparently larger, such as the North East, there is still considerable pressure on the available stock.

There are also regional differences in the size and type of social rented dwellings. The differences are most marked in London, which consistently stands out as different from the other regions. A lack of larger social units results in more overcrowding (as measured by the bedroom standard[2]) in London. More than 12 per cent of social rented households in London are overcrowded, compared with approximately 3 per cent in the three northern regions. Households in the North and the Midlands are the most likely to have a spare bedroom, although the majority of households in all regions are living in dwellings that match their need, according to the bedroom standard. In contrast, most owner-occupiers live in dwellings with more bedrooms than they would need by this definition.

---

[2] The bedroom standard is a normative measure of occupation density, based on the ages and composition of the household, developed by the Government Social Survey in the 1960s.

Figure 10: Overcrowding in social housing – difference from 'bedroom standard'

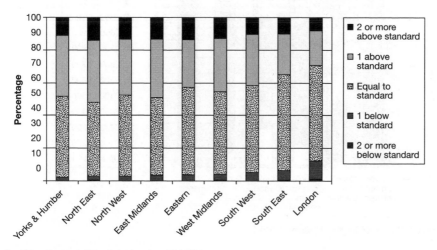

Source: Survey of English Housing 2005/06.

Economic impacts on demand

Only a small proportion of owner-occupiers want social housing (although that is still a very large number), while many more private renters do. However, most private renters who would like to live in social housing do not apply. In some cases this is because they think they would not have a high enough priority, but in many cases it is because they see their long-term future in owner occupation. Better-educated and childless people are the least likely to consider social housing.

Poverty is a major factor affecting the need for social housing. Higher poverty rates among BME populations increase their demand for social rented housing. The proportion of social renting households with a full-time worker has continued to fall, but incomes of social tenants in full-time work have risen faster than those in owner occupation. This implies that a small proportion of better-off tenants have pushed up the average.

Figure 11: Weekly household income of social tenants by household type

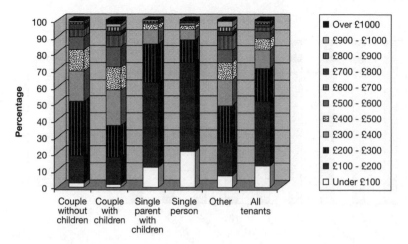

Source: Survey of English Housing 2005/06.

Most social tenant households have low incomes, with the majority earning (or receiving in benefits) between £100 and £300 a week. This differs substantially between couples and singles (including single parents) as couples are much more likely to have higher incomes. More than 30 per cent of couple households earn over £400 a week.

New entrants to social housing have low incomes and generally do not have anyone in full-time work. In contrast, over 70 per cent of those leaving the sector have one or more person in full-time employment, and their incomes are significantly higher than those who remain. However, the high cost of market housing has reduced the number of exits in recent years. This has reduced the supply of social units available for re-let.

One reason for the relative poverty of social tenants is their lack of economic activity. Economic status varies substantially between household types. Approximately 50 per cent of childless households are retired. As shown in Figure 12, opposite, of non-retired households, couples and 'other' household types have higher rates of employment than either single people or single parents. It is clearly difficult for single parents to find full-time employment that pays sufficiently to afford childcare, although significant numbers work part-time.

Figure 12: Economic activity of social tenants – employment status by household type

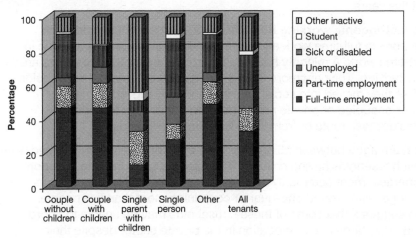

Source: Survey of English Housing 2005/06.

Main groups in social housing

Overall trends and averages often produce a stereotypical view of the average social housing tenant. In reality, social housing tenants are a hugely diverse group encompassing people from a wide range of backgrounds, although in different proportions from other tenures.

To help understand the diversity of residents, interviews were carried out with over 600 social tenants for this research.[3] A cluster analysis was used to help identify the main groups of residents living in social housing. This pointed to four identifiable clusters of residents:

- young urbanites
- modest-income working households
- non-working poor households
- older, settled households.

Young urbanites mostly live in London, and most of the rest in the South or East. Around one-half of this group are single people, and just under one-half have children. They are most likely to express dissatisfaction with their current accommodation, with around one-fifth saying that their home does not meet their needs very well, or not at all well. Most are young (under 35) and the majority of both Black and Asian residents are in this group. Their incomes are widely dispersed with higher numbers at both ends of the spectrum than the other groups.

---

[3] The interviews were carried out by British Market Research Bureau (BMRB) using their omnibus survey to ensure only eligible households were able to participate.

They are a significantly more mobile group than the others: over one-third had moved within the last year and the great majority had moved within the last five years.

Modest-income working households are largely households with someone in full-time work and most of the remainder have someone in part-time work. A minority have studied to the age of 21, and others are still studying. They are more likely to have been established households before they moved into social housing, and they moved from either owner-occupied or private rented housing rather than through the homelessness route or from living with family or friends.

Most are aged between 25 and 45. They are more likely to be married, with most households having children. They generally live in three-bedroom properties, most commonly semi-detached houses. Household sizes are large, with around one-quarter containing more than five people. This suggests that some of these households may be unable to afford adequately large accommodation in the private sector despite their moderate incomes.

A large majority (85 per cent) of these households have internet access. When asked what would most improve their home, this group was particularly likely to wish for additional rooms or more space, or dedicated parking. This may, in part, be because these are the largest households, and hence most likely to be overcrowded and need extra room. However, it may also be because, being somewhat better-off, though by no means wealthy, the aspirations of this group in housing terms are higher.

Non-working poor households, are similar to working households in terms of age, housing type and presence of children. However, they differ markedly in terms of income and employment status. More than two-thirds have incomes of under £10,000 and more than one-half under £6,000.

The vast majority of this group left school aged 16 or under. They are less likely than modest-income working households to be married, and more likely to be divorced, widowed or separated.

They are disproportionately congregated in the north of England and very small proportions of BME households are within this group. Most live in three-bedroom properties which are either terraced or semi-detached homes.

They are more likely than other groups to have moved to their current home directly from living with their parents, and reasons for entering social housing were often related to having children and needing a bigger home. Two-thirds of this group have lived in at least one other home within the social sector prior to moving to their current home. This group was particularly likely to want basic problems with windows, heating, internal decoration and maintenance addressed. Only one in four households in this group have internet access.

Older, settled households is the group that is most strongly differentiated from the others. The majority of this group are aged over 55, with most over 65. The largest group are therefore retired, with most of the remainder not in work. Almost none of these households have children and just over one-half are one-person households.

They are the least mobile group, and most have lived in their current home for over ten years. Around one-third are currently married, and nearly all of these have been married for over 20 years. However, the largest component of this group are divorced, separated or widowed. Very low numbers of BME households are within this group. Household incomes are low to moderate, almost all under £25,000.

Property size varies with a roughly even three-way split between one-, two- and three-bedroom properties. This group are much more likely than any other to live in bungalows but, nevertheless, larger numbers live in semis, terraces and flats. Most have moved to their current home from a previous social rented home, but significant numbers had moved from owner-occupation. They were also more likely than other groups to have moved for health-related reasons.

They are significantly more likely than the other groups to say that their current home meets their needs very well or quite well. This group was strikingly likely to say that 'nothing needs improving' about their current home – nearly half of all respondents gave this answer when asked what would most improve their house. This compares to around only one-quarter of respondents in the other three groups. Only one in eight of this group have internet access.

What sort of housing do social tenants want?

The omnibus survey, along with focus groups, allowed analysis of the kind of housing demanded by social tenants, and this can be compared with housing aspirations more generally.

Like the general population, social tenants expressed a desire for larger homes than they have at the moment, and this was associated with the number of children and particularly with those in the higher-income groups. Wanting a larger home often involved wanting a larger kitchen and living room as well as additional rooms. Open plan kitchen/living rooms were generally disliked.

Again, like the general population, social tenants prefer houses to flats and maisonettes, and this preference was also related to having children and to being better-off. Along with wanting a house, social tenants wanted a private garden so that children could play – and more housing association tenants expressed this preference than council tenants.

Social tenants were often dissatisfied with the design of their home and the standard of maintenance provided. This included particular dissatisfaction with noise insulation and ventilation, which aren't issues that have received much attention as priorities of home buyers.

Neighbourhood management is an issue for social tenants as it is for those in other tenures. Social renters are overall more likely to be dissatisfied with their area than other tenure groups.

Older social tenants expressed a desire for facilities and support in old age, although they were least likely to express dissatisfaction with their current home.

Overall, the analysis found that while residents of social housing share some of the desires and preferences of owner-occupiers, their priorities are not exactly the same. The desire for more indoor and outdoor space seems to be a strong theme across all tenure groups and household types, and to be especially an issue for families. Parking is also an issue in most central urban areas, irrespective of tenure.

However, there are many more issues surrounding the use and management of communal areas for social housing residents. There were examples where shared facilities were enhancing residents' lives, most notably in sheltered housing where older residents could find companionship with others like themselves at a time of life when they no longer belong to such a self-contained family unit. However, shared spaces can be very problematic for tenants, especially when different ages and household types are sharing. Different views surrounding where, when and how children should be playing, noise, dogs, and belongings left in stairwells can all become major issues for residents. These issues would seem to be of greater importance to social housing residents than some of the desires expressed by homeowners, such as for ensuite bathrooms and computer rooms.

Many of the issues relate to the physical attributes of the stock which would be difficult to change, but which could be addressed better in the design of new housing. Some relate to factors such as storage and noise which might be more easily addressed. Still others relate to lack of control over tenants' own environment and lack of autonomy in decision making. Again these may be susceptible to change.

Overcrowding and lack of space is a difficult issue to tackle while the housing stock is under such pressure overall. However, extensions and loft conversions, garden sheds or studios might offer some possibilities in some areas. More could also be done to make better use of existing stock by encouraging smaller older households to move to smaller housing, freeing up larger homes for young families. It is when children are young that families are more likely to want a garden; yet long waiting lists for transfers can mean families finally get one just as their children are entering their teens. Not many years later the children leave altogether.

Conclusion

There is no lack of demand for social housing. This implies that if supply were to increase in the right areas, it would quickly be taken up (see also Bramley, Chapter 8). It is currently constrained by people's perceptions of their chances of getting housed, the reality of long waiting lists, allocations criteria that prioritise certain groups of people, and in some cases a lack of knowledge about what is available.

Inflows and outflows to and from the social sector are unbalanced, those leaving tend to be those in employment while new entrants tend to be outside of the labour force. This makes it inevitable that the social sector is always providing help for those in the worst circumstances, even in less pressured areas. Movement in and out of the sector is slow and the resulting change in the profile of social tenants is gradual, not dramatic.

The over-representation of some BME groups, single women and lone parents, disabled, and economically inactive households is not a failing of social housing, but results from the difficulties these groups face in accessing any other housing. Improved access to private housing is the main measure that might reduce demand. But moves into home ownership have become more difficult so the profile may start to include more working households excluded from other choices.

Nonetheless, it would take a change in policy to create a more dramatic change in tenant profile. Expanding into the intermediate market would add more working households and younger childless households into the sector. However, the current policy emphasis on owner occupation and resultant decrease in the size of the social sector means it is unlikely that it will be able to focus on housing mainstream couples in employment, but rather the poor, those with special needs, and large families (who will increasingly be overcrowded). Moreover, there is no real demand from higher-income households who have other major opportunities available and can make their own decisions about where to live.

Regional differences in demand are now more about the extent of excess demand, rather than low demand as in the past. The South, and particularly London, is under the most pressure, although Yorkshire and Humberside also has high numbers on the housing register relative to the number of new lets available. Regionally, the main distinction is between London and the rest, with the profile of the other southern regions still more like the North and the Midlands than London. Notably, two-thirds of all households in temporary accommodation in England are located in the capital. There has been a general increase in overcrowding in the social sector in recent years, after a gradual decline that took place over the last 20 years, and again this is most acute in London.

Demand for social housing comes mainly from the poorest households, whereas better-off households are the most likely to leave the sector. Together, these two factors have caused a gradual residualisation of the sector over the last 25 years. There have been constantly falling numbers of economically active households, but this is not from a lack of demand from households on moderate incomes, but from a lack of supply to house them. The most pressing challenge lies in meeting and managing a higher demand than can currently be met.

Sarah Monk is Deputy Director of the Cambridge Centre for Housing and Planning Research and Senior Research Associate at the Department of Land Economy, University of Cambridge.

Anna Clarke is a Research Associate at the Cambridge Centre for Housing and Planning Research, University of Cambridge.

Christine Whitehead is Director of the Cambridge Centre for Housing and Planning Research, University of Cambridge and Professor of Housing in the Department of Economics at the London School of Economics.

Chapter 10

Conclusions

Suzanne Fitzpatrick and Mark Stephens

Introduction

The central thesis that prompted this book is that relatively good quality housing may represent a hidden asset for poorer people in England and the wider UK, and that this is a characteristic of the British welfare state that we should be concerned to protect. The review of European data presented by Bradshaw et al in Part 1 of the book concluded that this thesis could be upheld with some reservations – poorer households in the UK fared well with regards to several aspects of physical housing quality but badly with respect to perceived safety in the local area. The UK certainly did better on housing indicators than it does on most poverty league tables and so housing (although not the neighbourhoods in which much of it is situated) can be considered a comparative asset for poorer people in this country.

A key part of this housing and poverty 'story' in the UK is social housing, hence the focus of this book on the future of this sector. The book was intended, in part, as a corrective to the overwhelmingly negative portrayal of the social rented sector in recent years. It has been framed in the light of the debate generated by John Hills' (2007) independent review of the future roles of social housing in England for the Secretary of State for Communities and Local Government, and the Government's intention to produce a new Green Paper on housing reform by the end of 2008.

In Part 2 of the book it is argued that the continued existence of a substantial social rented sector, together with legal, policy and financial arrangements which ensure access to the mainstream parts of this sector to poorer households, has made a significant contribution to the achievement of these relatively good housing outcomes. Stephens (Chapter 2) contends that social housing acts as a vital safety net for poorer people in England and in the rest of the UK. While social housing now accommodates only 17 per cent of the population, it contains 39 per cent of households living in poverty (defined as having incomes of less than 60 per cent of the median after housing costs). Although social housing has been a diminishing tenure in the UK, and the policy debate surrounding it has emphasised its residual nature, it has been subject to rising expectations of standards over the years, with Decent Homes the latest and most ambitious of these programmes, as discussed below.

Fitzpatrick (Chapter 3) argues that the homelessness legislation is a crucial element of the legal frameworks that ensure access to social housing for poorer families, not least because its passage in 1977 marked a key component in the overall shift away from social housing allocations systems dominated by merit towards those based on need. Strictly speaking, the main homelessness duty is to secure temporary accommodation until suitable settled housing becomes available. However, in practice, this duty is almost always discharged through the offer of a social rented tenancy by the relevant local authority, which makes it far more difficult for these social landlords to exclude the poorest and most vulnerable households from the mainstream social rented sector than is the case in some other European countries. There is now robust quantitative evidence that the provision of assistance under this statutory framework is associated with substantial net improvements in the quality of life of homeless households, almost all of whom are poor, as well as being in acute housing need (Pleace et al 2008). Thus, indications that recent developments within the homelessness prevention agenda may be undermining access to statutory assistance in some parts of the country are concerning.

The third key housing policy instrument discussed in Part 2 as contributing to relatively good housing outcomes for poorer households is Housing Benefit (Kemp, Chapter 4) which, for all its faults, does ensure that some form of mainstream housing is affordable to even the poorest households in the UK. Kemp notes that Housing Benefit has grown in importance as general subsidies to the social rented sector have declined, and now contributes more than 85 per cent of the total. His analysis suggests that Housing Benefit performs its role as an in-work benefit less effectively than its role as an out-of-work benefit, as only around one-half of eligible low-paid tenants claim it. Kemp argues that cutting the taper to reduce the severity of the poverty trap associated with Housing Benefit would be poorly targeted and that resources might be more effectively targeted at minimising financial risks for those entering low-paid employment. Kemp suggests that it would be problematic to extend the Local Housing Allowance to the social rented sector, as social tenants have much less opportunity to make trade-offs between rent and quality than their private renter counterparts.

Part 3 of the book considers a range of problems with the current social housing settlement. Kintrea (Chapter 5) considers the role of social housing in contributing to spatial segregation of poorer households, and outlines a range of measures that could be taken to tackle this. Pawson (Chapter 6) addresses the problems associated with the lack of choice and bureaucratic paternalism within social housing, focusing, in particular, on the contribution of choice-based lettings schemes which he demonstrates have achieved some modest success with respect to empowering house-seekers and improving outcomes such as tenancy sustainment. Robinson (Chapter 7) analyses the alleged link between worklessness and social housing, finding that, while there are very high levels of worklessness in the social rented sector, these arise from the severe and multiple personal disadvantages that distance many tenants from the labour market. There is no evidence of an independent tenure effect on levels of worklessness, and only limited evidence of relevant area effects. Bramley (Chapter 8) focuses on the need for, and quality of, social housing, providing a menu of policies with regards to future supply. Monk et al (Chapter 9) examine the demand for social housing, arguing that it needs to be of the right type, place, tenure and price. They establish that while 'there is no shortage of demand for social housing' distinct demand groups exist with clear preferences for different types of housing.

A number of key themes and arguments run through these contributions to Part 3 of the book, some of which also appear in Part 2, and are drawn out in the discussion below:

- the supply of social rented housing

- the needs basis of social housing allocations

- security of tenure for social tenants

- the status of social housing, and

- neighbourhood conditions, area effects and mixed communities.

This final chapter of the book ends by reflecting on the current debate and the prospect of a new Green Paper on housing reform in the very near future.

The supply of social rented housing

It is now clear that there is a shortage of social housing in most parts of the country. Bramley's chapter examines this in detail, and his modelling work shows how worsening affordability in the home ownership sector has driven up demand for social renting, and that there is now a massive gap between need and supply of new affordable housing provision (ie social housing and low-cost home ownership). While pressures are greatest in London, projected increases in need are largest in proportionate terms in the North and Midlands. At the same time, the phenomenon of low demand for social rented housing, which affected many localities in the North and Midlands in the late 1990s, has dramatically reduced, though it has not been completely eliminated and may recur in some areas. The Government plans to raise output of new social rented housing provision to 45,000 per year in England by 2010/11, with at least 25,000 additional homes under shared ownership and shared equity schemes each year between 2008 and 2011. Indeed, 2007 witnessed the first growth in the social rented sector since 1980 as a consequence of a modest increase in the housing association development programme and the very much reduced levels of right to buy.

But, as the Bramley model indicates, the relatively modest planned increase in supply (even if achieved) will barely meet newly arising needs, and will fail to arrest – let alone tackle – the growing backlog in unmet housing needs (estimated at around one million units in 2006). Moreover, it is concerning that the credit crunch is already limiting social landlords' ability to produce new housing, not only because of the difficulties in accessing private finance but also because of their increased dependence on the health of the owner-occupied and shared ownership markets through section 106 agreements and the sale of dwellings to generate income to cross-subsidise rental development.

The adverse consequences of this shortfall in supply are picked up in a number of other chapters in the book. For example, Pawson notes the particular difficulties in offering 'real choice' to prospective social tenants inhigh demand areas. In some localities, very large numbers of bids are typically recorded for each advertised property, with reports of some adverts drawing up to 500 applications. In these circumstances, Pawson argues that publicly accessible advertising may be unjustifiably raising expectations for large numbers of people, and it may make sense to run choice-based lettings as a closed system open only to those above a certain priority threshold. This is clearly not ideal, and runs counter to current government policy: but where demand outstrips supply to this extent, it is perhaps the only viable way forward. In a similar vein, Fitzpatrick notes that the acute shortfall in social housing supply in London means that it is extremely difficult to move statutorily homeless households on to settled housing, necessitating lengthy stays in temporary accommodation which are a source of great frustration to the families involved and place large demands on the public purse. Given this, she argues that it may be necessary to consider unattractive, but possibly unavoidable, restrictions on statutory rights, such as tightening local connection rules in the capital.

Allocation based on housing need

A number of authors make the point that that the current safety net role played by the social rented sector in England and the wider UK should not be jeopardised by future policy or legal developments. Stephens argues that the safety net role of the social rented sector is suited to the relatively high levels of poverty and inequality in the UK and he demonstrates that in several other European countries '... the greater "income mixing" that is often regarded as being far superior to the UK system is achieved in part by the explicit exclusion of poorer and vulnerable households from the mainstream social rented sector' (p.34–35). This is not a policy approach that is likely to be considered acceptable within England or the wider UK.

It is undoubtedly the case that this continuing emphasis on meeting housing need, in combination with the restrictions on supply, puts a serious brake on other policy commitments, such as the promotion of mixed communities: 'Without spending on increasing the supply of social housing far beyond existing commitments... it is hard to see how an extension to more affluent groups could be justified.' (See Kintrea, p.75.) Likewise, Pawson makes the point that, while the primary safety net role of the social rented sector in this country can be seen as 'entirely logical', it is an important factor limiting the scope for a highly marketised approach where choice could play a dominant role, and where middle-income households could be accommodated in large numbers. Nonetheless, as Kintrea comments, meeting housing need continues to be the most convincing rationale for state intervention in the housing market, and therefore must be weighted heavily in any trade-offs with these other objectives.

Security of tenure

As noted by Bradshaw et al, the question of security of tenure for social tenants has received much attention recently, starting several years ago when the Cabinet Office apparently mooted the possibility that social housing should become a tenure of 'transition' rather than 'destination' (Fitzpatrick and Pawson 2007). More recently, press reports that the then Secretary of State for Communities and Local Government (Ruth Kelly) was planning to end security of tenure for social tenants generated so much controversy that John Hills opened his remarks at the launch of his review by saying:

> 'If you came here with the impression that I was going to be recommending the ending of security of tenure or that tenants will be thrown out of their homes then you're going to be disappointed.' (Quoted in Rashleigh 2007.)

Hills concluded that ending security of tenure would be an 'unhelpful disincentive' to moves towards economic independence, a point also made by Robinson in this book. Robinson emphasises the importance of the security and stability of the social rented sector for vulnerable tenants whose lives in other respects are in a state of flux. He argues that for those furthest from the labour market this security enables them to focus on other challenges in their lives, such as health or caring responsibilities, while for those closer to the labour market it facilitates their ability to secure and maintain employment. This means that any moves to undermine such security may impact adversely on levels of worklessness.

As Robinson details, the Minister for Housing, Caroline Flint, has linked the debate on security of tenure directly with incentives to tackle worklessness. She has suggested offering 'a complete package of incentives and opportunities along with the keys to their new home' (Flint 2008b) and asking, 'Could new tenants who can work sign commitment contracts when getting a tenancy, agreeing to actively seek work alongside better support?' (Flint 2008a). Few would disagree with the identification of disproportionate levels of worklessness among social tenants as a problem, and most would support the provision of support and training to assist workless households to gain employment, though they might question why it should be tenure-specific. Yet, by raising the issue of conditionality, the focus has become perilously narrow.

The idea raises both ethical and practical questions. While unemployment-related social security benefits have always been conditional on seeking (or at least availability for) work, there is no precedent for any of the principal benefits-in-kind (health, education or housing) that are unrelated to worklessness being subject to work-tests. Moreover, if conditionality in unemployment-related benefits is insufficient to secure employment, why should the threat of losing social housing be more effective? And if workless tenants are in receipt of sickness or disability-related benefits, then the problem might lie with the design of these benefits, although the Minister has indicated that conditionality would not be applied to 'the vulnerable like... those with disabilities' (Flint 2008b).

Other contributors to this volume argue that removing security of tenure would have other deleterious consequences, often at odds with stated government objectives. Thus, Pawson comments (p.99) that removing security of tenure would '...surely conflict with aspirations for social housing as a tenure of choice – both because households are less likely to choose to enter the tenure, and are also prevented from exercising the choice to stay in it'. Fitzpatrick raises particular concerns with regards to the impact on families with dependent children, citing evidence which suggests that the security of tenure offered by settled social housing is particularly important to both parents and children in families accepted as statutorily homeless (though much less so to 16-17 year olds accepted as homeless, probably reflecting their very early stage in their housing career).

This debate seems far from over, however, and we must remain alert to the possible undermining of the security of tenure of social tenants in future legislation, as all evidence indicates this would be a most retrograde step.

The status of social housing

The relative esteem and attractiveness of social housing is a recurring theme throughout the book, but here various authors seem to differ in their views, or at least in their emphasis. Thus Pawson (p.85) refers to '... the evolution of a progressively more residualised social housing sector, a tenure of last resort increasingly occupied only by those with no other choice,' and Kintrea makes very similar comments. Contrast this with Robinson's findings (p.110) that social tenants often emphasised a range of benefits of living in the sector, including security of tenure and the right to buy, though seldom the work-related benefits of sub-market rents:

'Contrary to a popular perception that social housing is a tired brand, a relic of a bygone era of welfare provision... there was near universal agreement among the social tenants (and many of the private tenants) interviewed that the sector provides a superior residential offer than the private rented sector for people on low incomes.'

To some extent, these apparent differences are explained by the *point of comparison:* Robinson is explicitly contrasting social housing with the private rented sector, whereas, given the widespread aspiration towards home ownership and its dominant position in the housing system, most analyses of the relative unpopularity of social tenancies implicitly take owner occupation as their point of comparison. Certainly, the relative popularity of social housing, as compared with private renting, fits with the reluctance of many statutorily homeless households to accept offers in the private rented sector, 'holding out' for a social tenancy instead (see Fitzpatrick). Likewise, note the evidence presented by Monk et al that a substantial number of private renters would like a social tenancy. Also relevant here is *whose* views are being considered: while for the general population social housing may no longer be an attractive option, for many poorer households it may provide not only a better deal than the bottom end of the private rented sector, but may also have advantages over marginal home ownership, something that is likely to become more apparent as house prices fall and repossessions rise (Stephens et al 2008). The idea that social housing is irredeemably unpopular also sits uneasily with the evidence provided in this volume about demand for social tenancies far outstripping supply in many parts of the country (see, in particular, Bramley and Monk et al), although it could be argued that this doesn't necessarily mean that the sector is popular, just that a great many people have no better or viable alternatives.

All that said, there is considerable evidence of the stigma that now attaches to residence in the sector (Kemp 2000), and there can be little doubt that this has increased in recent years, as the sector has shrunk and poorer and workless households have become increasingly concentrated within it. To a large extent this 'residualisation' is an unwelcome corollary of the sector's primary function as a safety net in which the meeting of housing need is prioritised. Moreover, as Kintrea points out, while social housing has undoubtedly downshifted in terms of tenants' social status and income over the years, and this is matter of regret insofar as it negatively impacts on current tenants, '... it is remiss to overlook that, in its heyday, access to council housing was selective, often discriminatory, and did not readily house many of those in the strongest needs' (p.78).

Bramley suggests that there may be some grounds for optimism looking forward. In particular, he highlights the major and sustained drive to bring the social housing stock up to the Decent Homes Standard by 2010, and highlights that between 1996 and 2005 there was a 45 per cent reduction in non-decent homes in the social rented sector: a rate of improvement that was greater than in the private sector, leading to the prospect that the relative position and attractiveness of the social sector may improve over time. However, as Bramley also notes, improvements in physical standards are not by themselves sufficient; neighbourhood social conditions and associated environmental problems remain a considerable concern, as now discussed.

Neighbourhood conditions, area effects and mixed communities

A credible case could be made that the most profound, and intractable, problem with the current social housing settlement in England and the wider UK is poor neighbourhood conditions. Certainly there is strong evidence that social tenants are more dissatisfied with (see Bramley), and fearful in (see Bradshaw et al), their neighbourhoods than other households, and that these negative effects are associated with the concentration of poverty in many of the areas in which social renting is located. In theory, social housing should help to counter the income segregation that is the natural tendency of market allocation processes but, as both Kintrea and Bramley point out, the opposite is the case. This is, in part, a continuing effect of historic building patterns, with much social housing remaining on bounded, large estates but, as Bramley highlights, current building patterns still tend to concentrate new social housing provision in the most deprived wards, even though demand is weakest there.

It is a considerable step from recognising the unpopularity of areas of concentrated poverty and social housing, to assuming that such areas generate *additional disadvantages* which impact negatively on the life chances of those who reside there. Kintrea acknowledges that the evidence on the existence or otherwise of such area effects is mixed in the UK – a number of qualitative studies have found that such effects are real, although difficulties have been encountered in generating adequate statistical data to measure them. He nonetheless concludes that the international evidence does tend to support the view that there are good equity grounds for attempting to desegregate poverty. With respect to the area effects on levels of worklessness, however, Robinson is very cautious. His qualitative evidence suggested that there was no cultural resistance to work on the part of social tenants, although there was evidence of social norms and routines that represented barriers to formal paid work, as well as narrow spatial horizons among some local residents which restricted travel to work areas. However, multiple area effects were identified in only one of the four areas of concentrated social housing Robinson studied, and even here they were secondary to the impact of the profound personal labour market disadvantages their interviewees faced.

Thus, as Kintrea says, the matter is far from settled, and there is a need for better evidence from England and elsewhere in the UK, but most policy makers accept there is something in the area effects argument, hence the strong emphasis in Hills' report on creating 'genuinely mixed communities'. Whether mixed communities policies will deliver benefits to poorer people remains to be seen. Robinson for one is highly sceptical. But Kintrea contends that there is now clear evidence that master-planned mixed communities, for example, can work. He argues, looking at ways forward, that 'there is much to play for' with regards to desegregating poverty – and we tend to agree.

The current debate and the Green Paper

As a new Green Paper on housing reform is drafted it is worth reflecting on past experiences. In 2005, the Government published the findings of an independent review of English housing policy that it had commissioned. The review, conducted by a team of 16 academics, was a systematic examination of housing policies over a period of a quarter of a century. It identified achievements, but also problems, including the concentration of worklessness among social tenants. In drawing out lessons for the future, the review identified some reasons why many problems remain outstanding and these included the tendency for policies to be *'narrowly conceived* because they deal with the symptoms of particular problems and ignore wider contextual differences,' and that 'emerging challenges remain unanticipated because policies are formulated as *reactions* to particular problems' (Stephens et al 2005, p.11, emphasis in original).

These lessons are especially apposite when considering possible reforms to the social rented sector. We have seen that security of tenure, introduced with bi-partisan support in 1980, is one of the most valuable attributes of social housing, and one that is now rarely enjoyed in the private rented sector. We would suggest that a sensible *starting point* for improving the lives of tenants is to build on the sector's strengths, not add to its weaknesses any more than one would attempt to fix a chair with a wobbly leg by kicking the leg away. Housing reforms over the past decade have improved the quality of the existing stock, but have neglected its supply and this has contributed to the acute allocation dilemmas in much of the country. The Government accepts that the answer is to increase supply, but with much more regard to the type and location of housing than has been the case in the past, including the promotion of more mixed communities. The Government has also attempted to make social housing more responsive to tenants' needs and to make choices more market-like, albeit that progress with this objective has been compromised by the sector's continuing safety net function.

These achievements are likely to be challenged as the economic environment deteriorates. As we have noted, the credit crunch has affected social landlords' ability to raise funds to support development programmes, and is affecting the ability of some housing associations to fund new build through shared ownership sales. More fundamentally, it has already shifted political attention to the worsening situation in the owner-occupied sector, as house prices fall and repossessions rise. A responsive housing market package has been announced in which the affordable housing programme is to be used to purchase unsellable developments that were intended primarily for the open market. This policy is likely to have unintended consequences, possibly good as well as bad. Unemployment has just risen at the fastest monthly rate since 1992 and, if it continues to rise significantly and adopts a strongly cyclical character, active labour market policies aimed at the activation of individuals are likely to become markedly less effective. While we might all aspire for the social rented sector to be more than a safety net, the value of this function seems likely to become even more evident than it is today.

References

Flint, C., 2008a. Address to the Fabian Society, Future of Housing. Conference, London. 5 Feb. Available at: http://tinyurl.com/5m7vaf

Flint, C., 2008b. Social housing and life chances. New Statesman online. 12 Feb. Available at: http://tinyurl.com/6yzrw6

Flint, C., 2008c. Speech delivered to Chartered Institute of Housing (CIH) Conference and Exhibition 2008. Harrogate International Conference Centre. 17 Jun. Available at: http://tinyurl.com/6zjhdh

Hills, J., 2007. *Ends and means: the future roles of social housing in England.* CASE Report 34, London: CASE and LSE. Available at: http://tinyurl.com/24ms5b

Kemp, P.A., 2000. Images of council housing. In R. Jowell et al., eds. *British social attitudes: the 17th report – focusing on diversity.* London: Sage, p.137–154.

Pleace, N., Fitzpatrick, S., Johnsen, S., Quilgars, D. and Sanderson, D., 2008. *Statutory homelessness in England: the experience of families and 16-17 year olds.* London: CLG.

Rashleigh, B., 2007. Hills reaction. *ROOF* online, 21 Feb. Available at: http://tinyurl.com/6d8zyc

Stephens, M., Whitehead, C. and Munro, M., 2005. *Lessons from the past, challenges for the future for housing policy: an evaluation of English housing policy 1975-2000.* London: ODPM. Available at: http://tinyurl.com/5p6off

Stephens, M., ed., Ford, J., Spencer, P., Wallace, A., Wilcox, S. and Williams, P., 2008. *Housing market recessions and sustainable home-ownership.* York: JRF.

List of abbreviations

BME Black and minority ethnic

CASE Centre for Analysis of Social Exclusion

CCHPR Cambridge Centre for Housing and Planning Research

CIH Chartered Institute of Housing

CLG Communities and Local Government

CML The Council of Mortgage Lenders

CORE The Continuous Recording System

DCLG Department for Communities and Local Government (now CLG)

DETR Department of the Environment, Transport and the Regions

DoH Department of Health

DSS Department for Social Security

DWP Department for Work and Pensions

EU15 Countries that were members of the EU before May 2004

FEANTSA European Federation of Organisations Working with the Homeless

HMSO Her Majesty's Stationary Office (TSO since 1996 (see below))

IPPR Institute for Public Policy Research

JRF Joseph Rowntree Foundation

LSE London School of Economics and Political Science

NHPAU National Housing and Planning Advice Unit

ODPM Office of the Deputy Prime Minister (now CLG)

OECD Organisation for Economic Co-operation and Development

OUP Oxford University Press

SEU Social Exclusion Unit

TSO The Stationary Office (privatised from HMSO since 1996)

YPS York Publishing Services

Index